ASSESSING RISK ON WALL STREET

Thomas A. Rorro

Published by: SOBARO Publishing Company
7855 Colonial Village Row
Annandale, VA 22003

Distributed to the book trade by: Liberty Publishing Company
50 Scott Adam Road
Cockeysville, MD 21030

Library of Congress Number: 83-51720

ISBN: 0-89709-134-5

To Rose and Jules
for a lifetime of help and encouragement

ACKNOWLEDGMENT.

This work represents a crossing of technical boundaries through the application of engineering principles to the stock market. Engineers have long been involved with the translation of mathematical principles into usable forms with concrete results. This work represents an engineering of the market place to provide an assessment of risk. Such a step cannot be made without the assistance of several individuals with complimentary areas of expertise. While help came from many, a few deserve special recognition.

The seed for this work was planted by Mr. Donald T. Mesler, a one time engineering associate who has left engineering to become an investment advisor. Assistance with the interpretation of the theoretical works was provided by Dr. Douglas C. Pearce. Finally, Mr. Robert Soto and Mr. Arthur Ballant, Jr., both long time friends, helped bring the document together in a structural and grammatical sense. To these individuals and others not mentioned, I offer my sincere thanks.

TABLE OF CONTENTS.

LIST OF FIGURES.

LIST OF FIGURES.

LIST OF TABLES.

LIST OF TABLES.

FOREWORD

A few exceptionally gifted individuals extract profits from the market on a regular basis. They are endowed with a special lobe in their brain denied to the rest of us. For everyone else, the market is perverse. Most participants pay tuition in the form of market losses to learn that forecasting is an art, not a science; that market newsletters are not infallible; and that the claims of yesterdays winners are difficult to match.

To the uninitiated, playing the game appears to be a trivial exercise. Simply latch on to the solid up-trends which seem so evident in the charts of stock prices. The reward should be instant gratification measured in dollars and cents and the chips can be cashed in at any time.

Neophytes soon learn that these trends are elusive. What's more, academic research suggests that they do not even exist. The academic community would argue that a succession of positive stock price changes is no more likely than a string of heads in a coin toss.

One market professional described organized securities exchanges as legal institutions for transferring wealth from the unsophisticated to the sophisticated. Can the average investor, who typically has a full time job in an unrelated field, compete in this environment? The answer is yes, but it means that his investment tools must be superior to those of the competition. It also means that his investment approach, perhaps even the investment vehicle, must be chosen with care. Doing what everyone else is doing with the expectation of being a winner may be overly optimistic.

A recent advertisement in an investment periodical makes an observation with uncanny insight. It suggests that an investor who is not using a computer is very likely entering into a transaction with a person who is. Assuming skillful exploitation of the computer's capabilities, why shouldn't the computerized investor have an edge?

Powerful tools, in the form of rigorous analytical techniques coupled with a computer, can be considered mandatory for investment success. Discipline will triumph over rules-of-thumb and seat-of-the-pants decisions. The computer makes implementation of even the most complex strategies conceivable. Without its number crunching capabilities it would not be possible to search through the myriad of alternatives to ferret out the select few promising situations. But let us not think of computers in some magical terms. The key to selection of an investment is the evaluation of its risk and its return. There need be no magic in this analysis. Placing things in perspective, it is of little value to discover a bad investment after it is made.

This is the approach that Thomas Rorro has mastered in his investment program. In his analysis of the broad spectrum of Stocks, Options and Convertible securities, the author has targeted an overlooked niche in the market place. By combining Convertibles with other securities in a technique called hedging, superior investments can be forged. To ferret out the promising situations he has applied powerful statistical techniques to determine the risk and expected profit of candidate investment situations. The investor is provided with the tools necessary to make investments decisions on a comparative basis one to another and to include the risk free money market rate. The necessary calculations are presented in a complete and concise form which facilitate their programming on a computer.

The final product is a rigorous and elegant investment technique. This technique provides the investor with the ability to assess the risk of an investment up-front where it counts. The approach is not pabulum. It will tax the intellectual resources of people trained to think in scientific terms and familiar with the manipulation of numbers.

Is it worth the bother? The logic of the approach and the demonstrated performance suggest that it is.

But can it survive the acid test in the real world with real dollars? Again, the author does not let us down here either. Unlike most investment books, *Assessing Risk on Wall Street*, includes a track record. This is the ultimate test of any system. Remarkably the performance results match the risk and profit goals chosen as the selection criteria. The analytical tools can be applied equally well to investments which are agressive or conservative at the investor's option. This technique demonstrates that investments, properly selected, perform magnificently!

This book is very well written and makes the best of a difficult subject but it will not appeal to everyone. The knowledge contained herein cannot be distilled into monosyllables and simple sentences. However, those who take the time to master its contents will be well rewarded.

And who knows? On the next trade, my computer may be competing against yours.

Donald T. Mesler
Chicago, Illinois

Mr. Donald T. Mesler is a Senior Vice President at Noddings, Calamos and Associates Inc., a Chicago based investment firm. He has been hedging convertible securities with stocks and options for more than fifteen years. His technical background provides a mesh between theoretical analysis and the day-to-day implementation of hedging strategies. Mr. Mesler holds an MBA degree from the University of Chicago. He currently serves as the President of the Chicago Chapter of the American Association of Individual Investors (AAII) and is an active contributor to the AAII's monthly journal and educational workshop sessions. Mr. Mesler is also a technical consultant to several financial publishers.

INTRODUCTION

There are two extremes of investors in the market place. The first are the gamblers who participate for the excitement and challenge which comes from trying to beat the system. On the opposite end of the spectrum there are those who seek only to increase their wealth and participate solely for monetary gains.

Both types of investors measure success by the magnitude of their profits. Both buy and sell securities in an attempt to maximize their return. The difference between these two extremes is the profit with which they are satisfied and the degree of excitement they wish to extract from the market.

For the gambler, the potential for spectacular gains comes with the risk of spectacular losses. For the conservative investor, low risk investments provide only moderate gains. Between the two extremes are levels which provide opportunity for increased gain at the expense of increased risk.

The market is complicated for even the most sophisticated investor. While the large volume investor can transact business relatively inexpensively, he is constrained to deal only in highly liquid securities. Conversely, the small investor will pay more for each transaction but has the flexibility to move in and out of the market with relative ease. Because of these differences and other anomalies in the market place, securities are not always fairly valued. Both under-valued and over-valued situations exist in the market at any given point in time. The key to success in the market place is to recognize and exploit these inefficiencies. To accomplish this feat the investor must understand the characteristics of the securities, their associated risk along with their profit potential.

The normal approach applied to the security selection process does not provide a perspective from which to evaluate risk. It is the intent of this publication to provide this perspective, and with it a mechanism to exploit the market's inefficiencies.

DOCUMENT CONVENTIONS.

This tome contains several mathematical expressions which represent the processes discussed in the text. The equations are presented in a character oriented notation which is different from standard mathematical form. In the interest of clarity, when the form of the equation is complicated both the standard mathematical representation and the character oriented forms are provided. The character oriented notation used for mathematical operations are:

OPERATION	FUNCTION
**	Exponentiation
*	Multiplication
/	Division
+	Addition
-	Subtraction

In addition to the notation, parentheses are used in the equations to control the order in which the calculations are performed. The simple rule to evaluate an equation is to combine the numbers in the inner most parentheses first and then remove the parentheses for the next operation. For example:

ANSWER = SQRT (6 + (2 * 5))

ANSWER = SQRT (6 + 10)

ANSWER = SQRT (16)

ANSWER = 4

In the above example, "SQRT" represents the square root function performed on the combined result of the three input numbers. Initially, the reader may not be comfortable with this form of presentation. However, by working a few of the early examples it will be easy to better your understanding. If you have a personal computer at your disposal, you will note that this notation is compatible with standard BASIC constructs. It might also be helpful to use your computer to verify the results of the examples which will be presented in the text.

CHAPTER I

A PERSPECTIVE

1.1 THE MARKET PLACE.

The market is a structure through which securities are exchanged for financial consideration. In the finest capitalistic tradition, the rate at which this exchange occurs is set mutually and exclusively by the buyer and the seller. In theory, the market is designed to insure a fair and unencumbered transfer of securities between the buyer and the seller. Unfortunately, the unscrupulous investor has exploited the spirit of the regulations which govern the market place. This activity has caused the Securities and Exchange Commission to develop an ever more complicated set of regulations. The main thrust of their efforts is to insure a fair and stable market. There is however an unfortunate side effect, these regulations encumber the market transactions.

As an example, in the past it was possible to simply enter the market place at any time and execute a short sale. A short sale occurs when securities are borrowed from another investor and sold. Some investors with large capital assets abused this privilege by first generating some false bad news about a company and then executing a large volume of short sales. When the price was sufficiently depressed, these same investors would cover their short positions at a substantial profit and then take a large long position (i.e. purchase a large number of shares) in the security at the bargain prices. As the market realized that the bad news about the company was false, the price would rise to its original level. This would leave the unscrupulous investor with yet another profit on his now long position.

In order to protect the investor from this practice, the regulations were modified. They now require that an uncovered short sale can only be executed following an up tic (i.e. an upward move) in the price of the security. This prevents investors from manipulating the price of a security but at the same time it impedes the short sale of as little as 100 shares of stock.

The mechanism of the market place are complicated not only by the regulations which govern the transactions but also by the very nature of the securities and their interaction with the economy. There is an old saying that "no amount of planning can beat dumb luck." In the long run however, the odds must catch up with even the "lucky investor." To be consistently successful in the market, the investor must understand its mechanisms and be able to evaluate risk.

1.2 UNDERSTANDING THE PROBLEM.

In the long run, success in the market place can only be achieved by the investor who understands the problem. The goal of any investment strategy is to turn a profit. The problem then is one of selection and timing. Selection is the process of picking from the myriad of available securities and timing is the control of when to enter or exit a position.

> Let us define an experiment as the selection and purchase of a security.

The outcome of such an experiment can be either profitable or unprofitable. It can, therefore, be assumed that participation in the market involves a degree of risk. The key issue in this experiment can be defined as the selection of a security which optimizes the potential for profit as a function of risk. If the selection is made under maximum profit and minimum risk conditions the result of many such experiments will be a profit. Time considerations fall out almost automatically by defining an acceptable level of profit balanced against the potential to reach that level.

1.3 THE MEASURE OF SUCCESS.

The investor may be described in many ways, but in the final analysis, he or she is human. His pride will lead him to boast about his many victories while mumbling about his defeats. It is the nature of the human animal to remember the good times and to justify and forget the bad times. To approach the market in a scientific manner requires that the analysis must be performed without this bias. The results of any valid analysis must show success, as well as failure, with the same clarity. As an intelligent investor you must insist on this treatment. To do otherwise is to hide your head in the sand.

To better explain the situation, let us consider the purchase of a new automobile for the sum of $8800.00. Since you have that amount in cash, you have the option to pay cash for the car or buy it on time payments. An aggressive salesman might insist that it is better for you to buy the car on time. His argument might go something like this:

> "If you pay $800.00 down, your monthly payments for 24 months on the $8000.00 balance is $369.16 given an interest rate of 10%. The total you will pay over the duration of the loan is $8859.83. If at the same time you leave your $8000.00 in the bank account at 6% interest, compounded monthly, your balance after 24 months will be $9017.28. Since this sum is in excess of the total you paid by $157.45, the time payments are to your benefit."

The argument is valid for as far as it goes but it does not represent an unbiased assessment of the situation. The comparison does not account for the monies you would have used for the payments given that you paid cash for the automobile. If you pay cash and deposit the monthly payment of $369.16 in your 6% account, your balance after 24 months will be $9388.46 which is $371.18 larger than the time payment approach. The comparison in order to be valid must be made against your net worth at the conclusion of the transaction. In this example, your net worth is a two year old car and the balance in your bank account. It is obvious on this basis that you are far better off to pay cash and run your own savings plan. The salesman is selling you a car and a forced saving plan. If you have no need for the latter, why buy it?

1.4 THE BOTTOM LINE IS PROFIT.

It is critical for the investor to approach the market without bias. The bottom line in any market transaction must include all costs incurred in performing the transaction. The unit of measure must be universally applicable over diverse investment techniques. The selected security must not only prove superior to other securities but also to other investment vehicles. The only desirable result is a profit. If the investor cannot extract a profit from the stock market there is no reason to participate. What the investor needs is an unbiased method to assess the potential for both profitability and risk.

1.5 TO PLAY THE GAME.

The all important assessment of profitability potential of a security is generally addressed by two schools of market analysts. The fundamentalist studies the underlying worth of the security in question in an attempt to assess profitability potential directly. The technical analyst studies graphs of the price and volume data in an attempt to recognize trends and predict the future.

Both the fundamental and technical approaches have merit but neither can categorize the inherent risk in an investment. A basic yet often unstated assumption of both approaches is that if it is followed rigorously, the risk is small.

Both approaches can be challenged. The fundamentalist can be confronted on the basis that stocks are not always valued according to the net worth of the underlying company. The technical analyst can be challenged on the basis that he attempts to predict the future. This is a feat considered impossible in most academic circles.

There is a need for a third category of analyst, the agnostic. He neither claims to predict the future nor cares about the minute details of the corporation. His concern is directed to a security only to the extent that it is an instrument for profit. The agnostic performs fundamental analysis to avoid companies which are candidates for bankruptcy and technical analysis to describe a broad band of possible prices for a security. He seeks to quantify the risk and then to maximize the ratio of profitability potential and risk. It is with this prospective that we proceed to evaluate the worth of individual investments.

CHAPTER II

THE BASIC BUILDING BLOCKS

2.1 MARKET INSTRUMENTS.

A portfolio is a complicated entity. The relationship of securities within it can generate a tangled web which, at first, appears impossible to comprehend. The key to understanding and evaluating a portfolio lies with the basic building blocks which comprise its structure.

Of the myriad of potential investment instruments, four types are of particular interest. These are: the common stock, the call option, the put option, and the convertible security. These securities are uniquely different yet similar in two respects. First, the value of each is tied directly to the price of its underlying common stock. Second, each instrument has a defined ability to generate a profit.

In order to fully understand the nature of market instruments they must be evaluated against common scales. These units of comparison are common stock price and profitability.

2.2 THE COMMON STOCK.

The common stock, by its basic nature, represents a share in the equity of the company of issue. It entitles the investor to a vote for the Board of Directors and a limited participation in other corporate decisions.

In good times, the investor profits from the company's financial growth. This is achieved through dividends and through the increased value of his share of the corporate equity. In bad times, the investor will also participate in fiscal crisis but only to the limit of his investment in the company.

> As an example, let us assume that an investor purchases 100 shares of XYZ common for $4.00 per share.

If the price rises to $10.00 the investor will have growth in his equity of 150%. In principle there is no limit on the price to which a stock might rise. Conversely, if the company went bankrupt, the maximum loss to the investor is his original investment of $400.00.

It would be relatively convenient if the value of common stock were determined by dividing the companies net equity by the number of shares outstanding. In practice however, the corporate equity is but one of many factors which determine the value of a share of stock. The nature of these factors is the subject of continuing debate. Yet, in spite of the controversy, the market is able to fix the price on every security.

For centuries, men have sought the elusive formula of success. If an investor were able to predict the future price of a single security, it would unlock, for him, unlimited wealth.

While the quest for this magic formula might be exhilarating to pursue, the investor is best advised to place his efforts to predict the future aside. His energy is best applied to analyzing the available and proven relationships between securities.

The value of any market instrument can be measured against the price of the underlying common stock. In the simplest case, the final value of an investment in common stock is the sum of the sale price of the stock plus any dividends accrued during the holding period multiplied by the number of shares held. This relates, in practical terms, to the amount of cash you put back into your pocket after an investment is liquidated.

The use of final value as a measure of the worth of an investment is the first and simplest extension in the process of investment evaluation. Since it is possible to compute the final value of an investment as a function of the price of the underlying stock, final value calculations represent the first step on the path to evaluating an investment's potential.

> As an example, let us assume that an investor purchases 100 shares of XYZ company at $10.00 per share. XYZ company pays a dividend of 50 cents per share annually.

The problem then is to calculate the final value of the investment after one year. Since the statement does not define the price of XYZ common at the end of the year, there are many solutions to this problem. To achieve an appreciation of the possible outcomes, it is useful to assume a common stock price and solve for the final value. This process can be extended to several assumed stock prices and will result in the data displayed in Table 1.

While a tabular display provides a useful view of the final value results, the basic nature of the final value result is best presented in graphical form. By plotting final value against assumed stock price it is possible to obtain a different perspective of the possible outcome. Figure 1 displays this final value curve. It is important to note that a final value curve can be generated for any of the four securities of interest. *But more important, it can be generated before the security is purchased giving the investor a new perspective on what the future might hold.*

While final value is a useful measure, it is the profit potential which is of greatest interest. In order to calculate profit, the investor need only subtract the initial cost of the investment from its final value.*

---

*Note: In the interest of clarity, all calculations are performed without the consideration of commission and margin interest charges. Accounting for these factors will be covered in Chapter 3.

TABLE 1. FINAL VALUE COMPUTATION FOR THE PURCHASE OF COMMON STOCK.

SHARES	ASSUMED PRICE	ANNUAL DIVIDEND	FINAL VALUE
100	$ 1.00	$0.50	$ 150.00
100	$ 3.00	$0.50	$ 350.00
100	$ 5.00	$0.50	$ 550.00
100	$ 7.00	$0.50	$ 750.00
100	$ 9.00	$0.50	$ 950.00
100	$11.00	$0.50	$1150.00
100	$13.00	$0.50	$1350.00
100	$15.00	$0.50	$1550.00
100	$18.00	$0.50	$1850.00
100	$21.00	$0.50	$2150.00

TRANSACTION: Buy 100 shares of XYZ company common stock at $10.00 per share with an annual dividend of 50 cents per share.

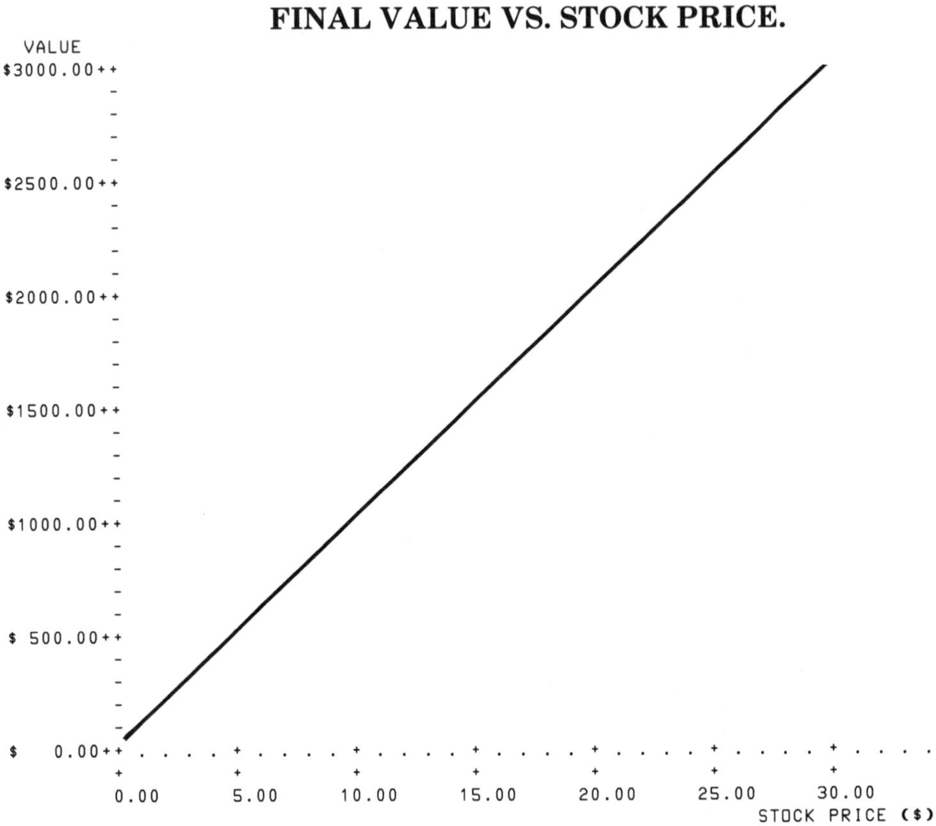

FIGURE 1. FINAL VALUE CURVE FOR THE PURCHASE OF COMMON STOCK.

TRANSACTION: Buy 100 shares of XYZ company common stock at $10.00 per share with an annual dividend of 50 cents per share.

In the previous example the cost of 100 shares at $10.00 per share is $1000.00. Combining the data in Table 1 with this initial cost yields a tabular listing of the profit potential of the investment which is contained in Table 2.

A careful review of Table 2 demonstrates that profit can be both positive or negative. This negative profit condition is also known as "loss." It is important to understand this representation of loss as a negative profit. The results listed in Table 2 can be depicted graphically as shown in Figure 2. The graphical representation provides the investor with a comprehensive picture of the profit potential.

The duration of the investment is an important factor in this example to the extent that the time period determines the value of the dividend earnings. Since the stock position can be held indefinitely, there is no absolute time limit. The holding period of one year was selected for convenience. It should be noted that the holding period is a constraint of expiring securities such as put and call options. For the present however, we simply note the selected time period.

The profit curve displayed in Figure 2 will be valid for the period over which it is defined. The usefulness of the graph lies in the fact that it represents a mathematical identity. It is in fact an indisputable statement of the profitability in the purchase of common stock.

There are financial considerations which will cause the graph to be modified before the holding period has expired. Special dividends and stock splits will cause a noticeable shift of the graph with respect to stock price. In the case of dividends the shift is usually small relative to the net profitability and in the case of splits the net profitability will remain unchanged.

TABLE 2. PROFIT COMPUTATION FOR THE PURCHASE OF COMMON STOCK.

ASSUMED PRICE	INITIAL COST	FINAL VALUE*	PROFIT
$ 1.00	$1000.00	$ 150.00	−$ 850.00
$ 3.00	$1000.00	$ 350.00	−$ 650.00
$ 5.00	$1000.00	$ 550.00	−$ 450.00
$ 7.00	$1000.00	$ 750.00	−$ 250.00
$ 9.00	$1000.00	$ 950.00	−$ 50.00
$11.00	$1000.00	$1150.00	+$ 150.00
$13.00	$1000.00	$1350.00	+$ 350.00
$15.00	$1000.00	$1550.00	+$ 550.00
$18.00	$1000.00	$1850.00	+$ 850.00
$21.00	$1000.00	$2150.00	+$1150.00

TRANSACTION: Buy 100 shares of XYZ company common stock at $10.00 per share with an annual dividend of 50 cents per share.

*Note: Final Value includes the annual dividend of 50 cents per share.

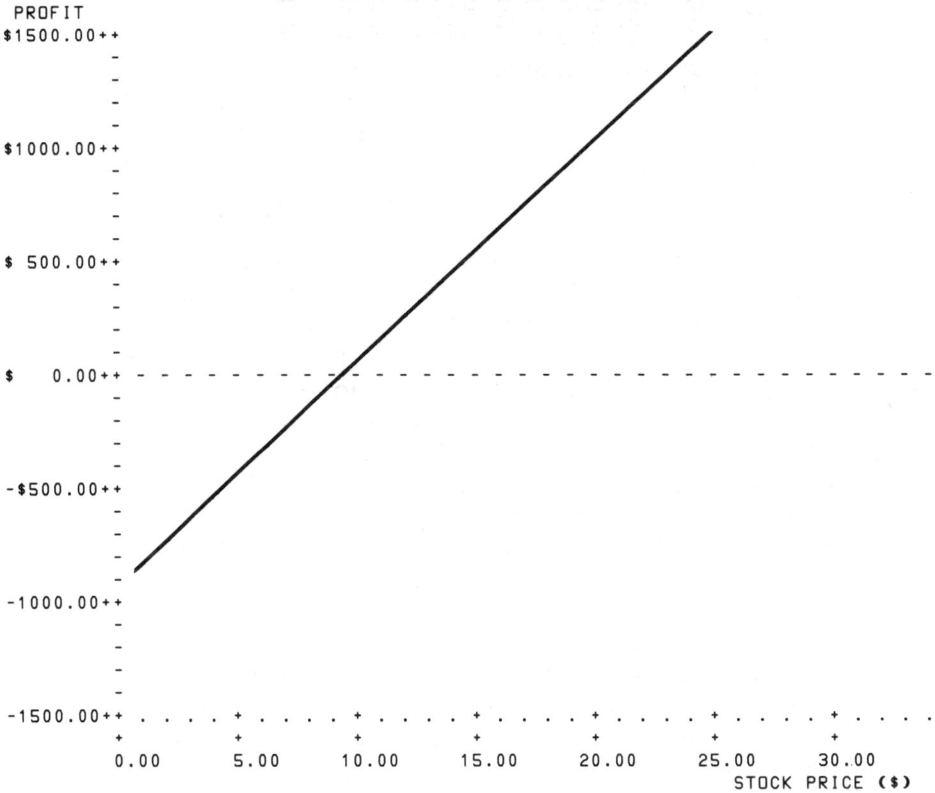

FIGURE 2. PROFIT CURVE AS A FUNCTION OF STOCK PRICE FOR THE PURCHASE OF COMMON STOCK.

TRANSACTION: Buy 100 shares of XYZ company common stock at $10.00 per share with an annual dividend of 50 cents per share.

Considering the case of a 2 for 1 stock split, the number of shares held will double but at the same time the price of the stock will halve. In effect then the slope of the profit curve will double and the curve will be shifted to the left by half the distance to the origin. The translation is linear and does not effect the net profitability of the position. It may be valuable to analyze a split condition. This is left as a exercise to the reader.

Beyond the straight purchase of common stock, it is also possible to execute a short sale. In this transaction, the investor borrows and sells the security (short). By so doing, the investor accepts the liability of any dividends paid by the company during the holding period of the short position and must at some time purchase and return the shares he has borrowed. Intuitively, the astute reader might conclude that the profit which the short investor realizes must be the inverse of the long investor's profit. In fact, this is a correct observation. The short investor profits as the underlying stock declines in price and incurs a loss if the stock price advances. In the former case the short investor can replace the subject securities for less than the price he received at the time of the short sale thus he realizes a profit. Conversely, if the stock price rises, he must pay a premium price to replace the shares he has borrowed. In either case the differences in the short sale price and the current price represents the net profit (or loss).

Table 3 displays the profit which will be realized for several assumed values of stock price for a short sale of common stock. A time period of one year is assumed in order to properly account for dividend liability. The graphical representation of Table 3 is displayed in Figure 3. A comparison of Figures 2 and 3 will provide the insight necessary to appreciate the profit relationship between the buyer and the short seller of common stock.

There are those who will argue that short sales of common stock are inherently a high risk. The intent here is simply to present the profit characteristics of an investment opportunity. Both the purchase and short sale have their place in the market. The reader is asked at this time, to simply note the existence of this investment situation and understand the profit characteristics.

TABLE 3. PROFIT COMPUTATIONS FOR THE SHORT SALE OF COMMON STOCK.

ASSUMED STOCK PRICE	INITIAL COST (received)	FINAL VALUE* (paid out)	PROFIT
$ 1.00	$1000.00	$ 150.00	+$ 850.00
$ 3.00	$1000.00	$ 350.00	+$ 650.00
$ 5.00	$1000.00	$ 550.00	+$ 450.00
$ 7.00	$1000.00	$ 750.00	+$ 250.00
$ 9.00	$1000.00	$ 950.00	+$ 50.00
$11.00	$1000.00	$1150.00	−$ 150.00
$13.00	$1000.00	$1350.00	−$ 350.00
$15.00	$1000.00	$1550.00	−$ 550.00
$18.00	$1000.00	$1850.00	−$ 850.00
$21.00	$1000.00	$2150.00	−$1150.00

TRANSACTION: Sell short 100 shares of XYZ company common stock at $10.00 per share with an annual dividend of 50 cents per share.

*Note: The final value includes the value of the annual dividend of $0.50 per share on 100 shares.

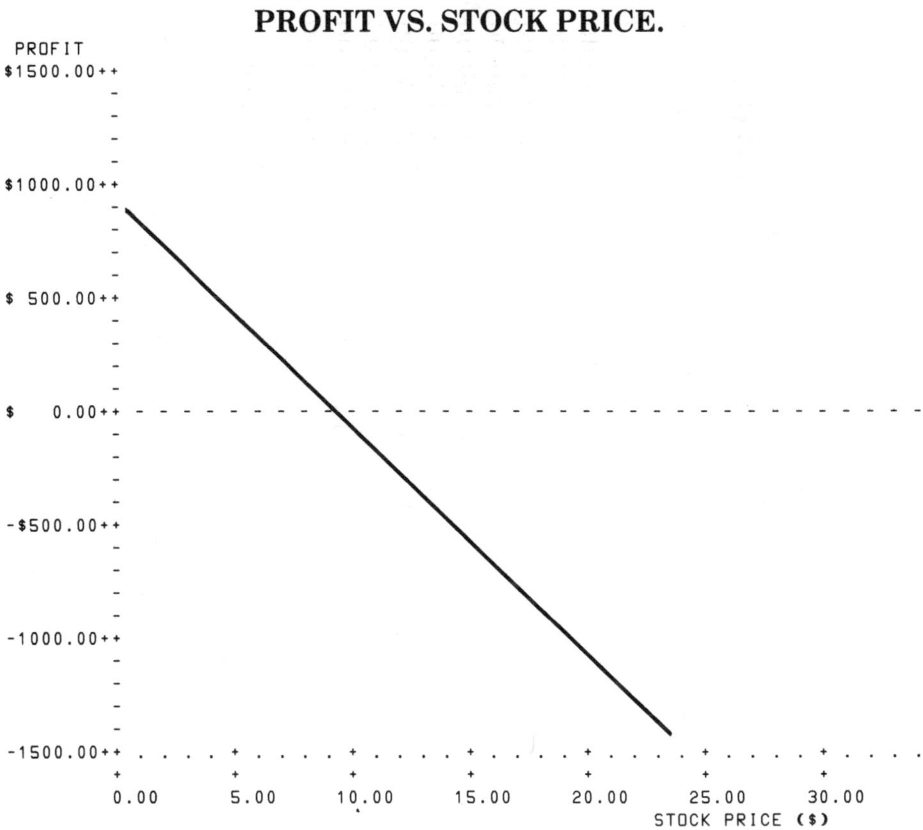

FIGURE 3. PROFIT CURVE FOR THE SHORT SALE OF COMMON STOCK.

TRANSACTION: Sell short 100 shares of XYZ company common stock at $10.00 per share with an annual dividend of 50 cents per share.

2.3 THE CALL OPTION.

The call option is the second type of security which is of interest. The call option is a contract between two parties which governs the exchange of a named security. The basis for the option was formed centuries ago to provide a means to reduce the risk of agricultural investments. Today, this same mechanism is available to the securities investor.

As with any agreement between individuals, it is possible to generate a private accord outside the structure of any market. In fact, until recently, options were bought and sold on just such a negotiated basis. When the Chicago Board of Options Exchange was created it provided a structured mechanism for options trading. Since its inception, the majority of all option trading takes place on a listed exchange.

A call option contract is an agreement between the buyer and the seller. The buyer receives the right to "call" (purchase) 100 shares of a named common stock at a specified price for a specified period of time. The seller agrees to provide the stock upon demand at that price to the option buyer. The key elements of an option contract are its purchase price, its exercise price and the duration (i.e. expiration date).

The purchase price of the call represents the total compensation to the seller. The buyer pays this premium for the rights which he receives. The specified expiration date makes the contract an expiring asset for the buyer and an expiring liability for the seller. The value of the call option at any point in time is a function of the exercise price, the current stock price and the time remaining.

To understand this relationship let us consider the potential value of the call contract as a function of stock price. An option to buy 100 shares of XYZ company at $10.00 per share must at least be worth $500.00 if XYZ company is selling for $15.00 per share. This is true because the holder of the option has the right to purchase 100 shares of the named stock at $5.00 below the market price. In addition, if there is time left on the option contract, the contract will sell for a premium over its intrinsic value. This premium is determined by the market's estimate of the probability that the stock will move higher before the expiration date of the option. The intrinsic or final value of an option represents a lower limit of its price. Given this fact, it is useful to evaluate this final value of an option contract as a function of stock price.

> Consider an option on 100 shares of XYZ common stock with an exercise price of $10.00.

Applying the logic stated above, the option's minimum value is the difference between the current stock price and the exercise price of the contract. If the stock is selling below the exercise price however, the option has an intrinsic value of zero. In simple terms, an investor would not pay for the right to purchase a stock for a price higher than its current market price, given that the right expires immediately after purchase of the option. It can be surmised then that the intrinsic value of an option below its exercise price is zero. The intrinsic value of an option above its exercise price is the difference between the current stock price and the exercise price of the option. A tabular display of the intrinsic or final value of an option contract is listed in Table 4.

Options do regularly sell above their intrinsic value. This is due to the time feature of the option contract. A premium is charged which is commensurate with the market's estimate of the probability that the stock will rise above the exercise price in the time remaining. Since as time passes there is less and less opportunity for the stock to rise in price, the option premium will decrease to zero as the option nears expiration. Figure 4 displays an example of the family of option value curves which converge on the intrinsic or final value.

TABLE 4. FINAL VALUE COMPUTATION FOR THE PURCHASE OF A CALL OPTION.

ASSUMED STOCK PRICE	INITIAL COST	FINAL VALUE	PROFIT
$ 1.00	$200.00	$ 0.00	−$ 200.00
$ 3.00	$200.00	$ 0.00	−$ 200.00
$ 5.00	$200.00	$ 0.00	−$ 200.00
$ 7.00	$200.00	$ 0.00	−$ 200.00
$ 9.00	$200.00	$ 0.00	−$ 200.00
$11.00	$200.00	$ 100.00	−$ 100.00
$13.00	$200.00	$ 300.00	+$ 100.00
$15.00	$200.00	$ 500.00	+$ 300.00
$18.00	$200.00	$ 800.00	+$ 500.00
$21.00	$200.00	$1100.00	+$ 900.00

TRANSACTION: Buy 1 call option on 100 shares of XYZ company common stock for $200.00 with an exercise price of $10.00.

OPTION VALUE VS. STOCK PRICE.

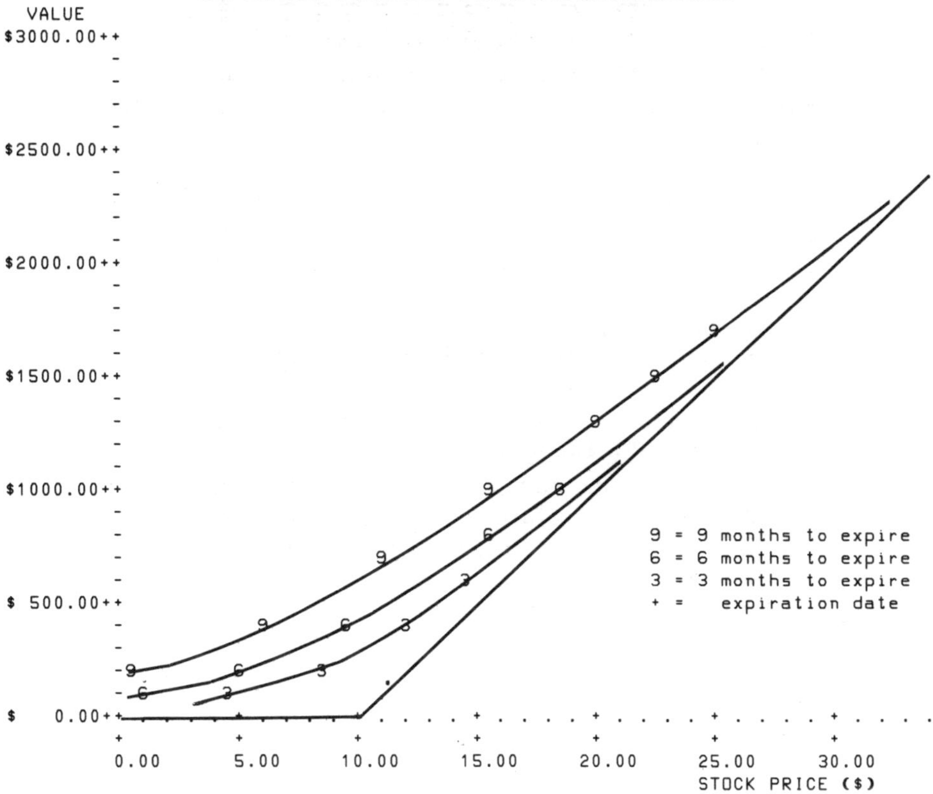

FIGURE 4. FAMILY OF OPTION VALUE CURVES FOR THE PURCHASE OF A CALL OPTION.

TRANSACTION: Buy 1 call option on 100 shares of XYZ company common stock for $200.00 with an exercise price of $10.00.

The profit to an option buyer on the day of its expiration is the difference between its final value and the purchase price. If the option were purchased for $200.00 some time prior to expiration, the profit on the day of expiration could be computed and the result is displayed graphically in Figure 5.

In this example, the buyer looses the $200.00 investment if the stock is selling below the exercise price on the day of expiration. The loss incurred is 100% of his investment. If the stock is selling for $5.00 above the exercise price the buyers gain is $500.00 less the $200.00 initial investment for a net profit of $300.00.

Since there are two sides to any transaction, when the buyer profits, the seller suffers a loss. The converse is also true. The profit curve of the seller is the inverse of the profit curve of the buyer. Figure 6 displays the final value profit curve of an option seller. Verification of this curve is left as an exercise to the reader.

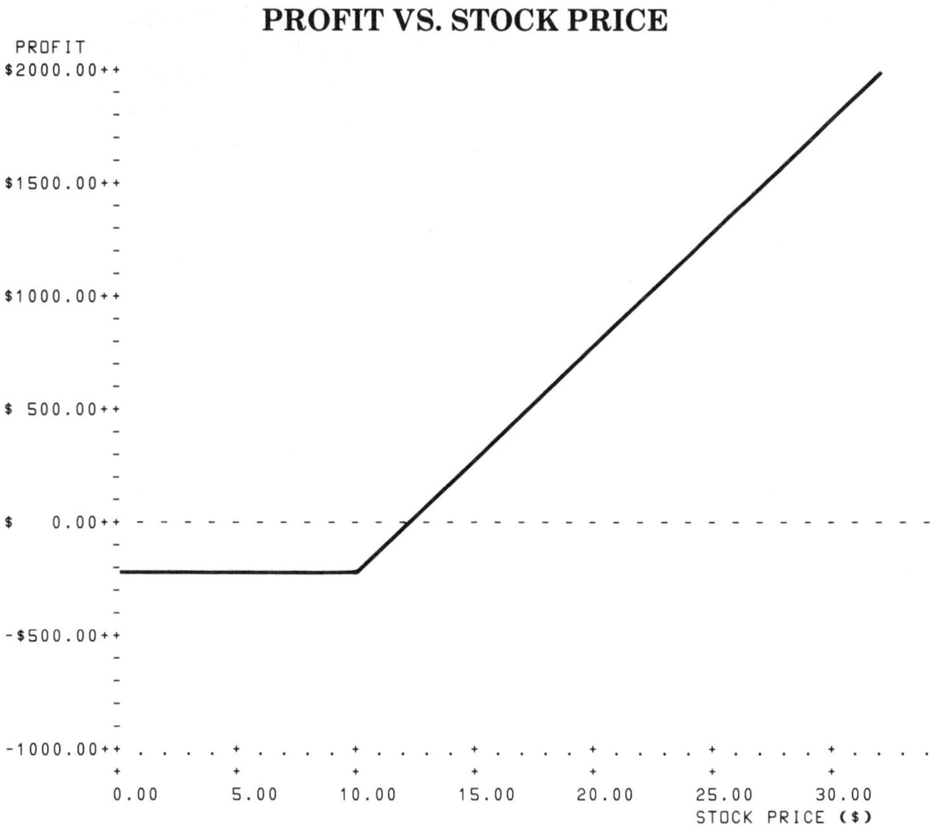

FIGURE 5. PROFIT CURVE FOR PURCHASE OF A CALL OPTION EVALUATED AT EXPIRATION.

TRANSACTION: Buy 1 call option on 100 shares of XYZ company common stock for $200.00 with an exercise price of $10.00.

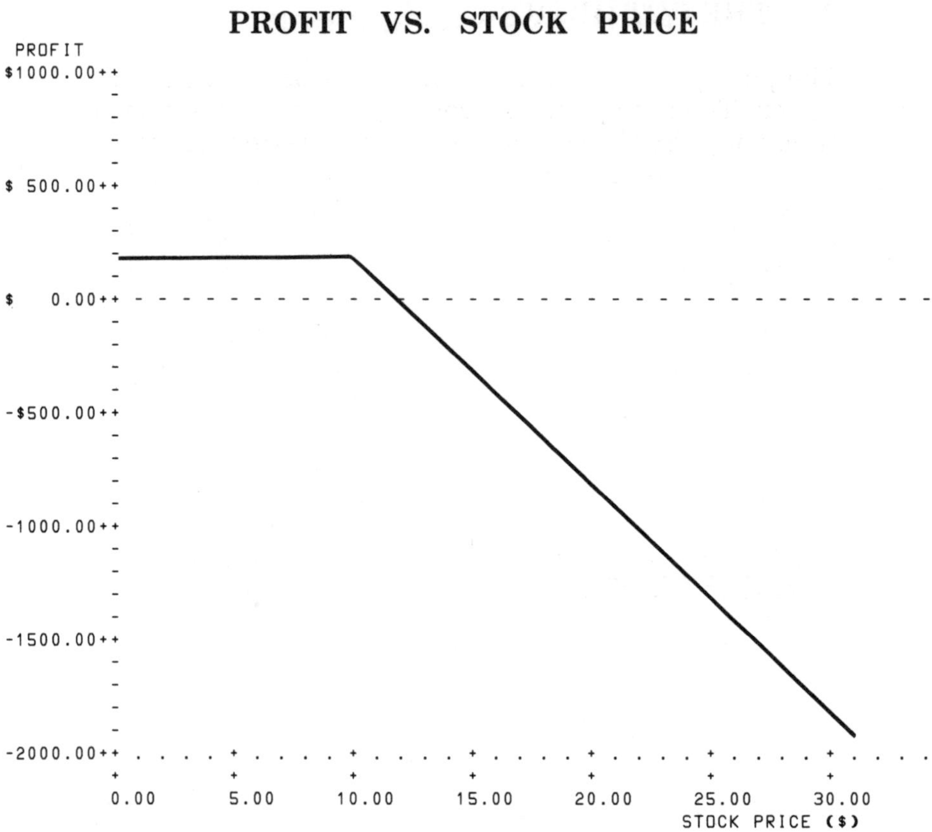

FIGURE 6. PROFIT CURVE FOR THE SHORT SALE OF A CALL OPTION EVALUATED AT EXPIRATION.

TRANSACTION: Sell short 1 call option on 100 shares of XYZ company common stock for $200.00 with an exercise price of $10.00.

2.4 THE PUT OPTION.

The put option is similar in many respects to the call option. The put option is a contract for a fixed period of time and, like the call option, it has a designated exercise price. The buyer of a put option purchases the right to sell (put) 100 shares of a specified common stock, to the put option seller, at a specified price for a specified period of time. Under the terms of the contract, the transfer of the securities occurs at the convenience of the put option buyer. Therefore, the put option seller must be ready and willing to purchase the stock at the specified price during the full term of the put contract.

The intrinsic value of the put option contract is a function of the price of the underlying common stock. At expiration, the right to put (sell) 100 shares of stock at $10.00 per share is of no value if the stock is selling for more than $10.00 on the open market. Conversely, a put option contract of $10.00 per share is worth $100.00 for each point the stock is selling below the exercise price of $10.00. Thus, a put option on 100 shares of XYZ company with an exercise price of $10.00 per share is worth $500.00 if the XYZ common stock is trading at $5.00 per share. Table 5 illustrates the intrinsic value of a put option as a function of stock price.

Like the call option, the put option sells at a premium over its intrinsic value. This premium is the market's estimate of the probability that the common stock will sell below the exercise price prior to expiration. As the time remaining for the contract decreases, so does the premium on the option contract. Figure 7 displays the put option value curves for various periods to expiration.

PUT OPTION VALUE VS. STOCK PRICE

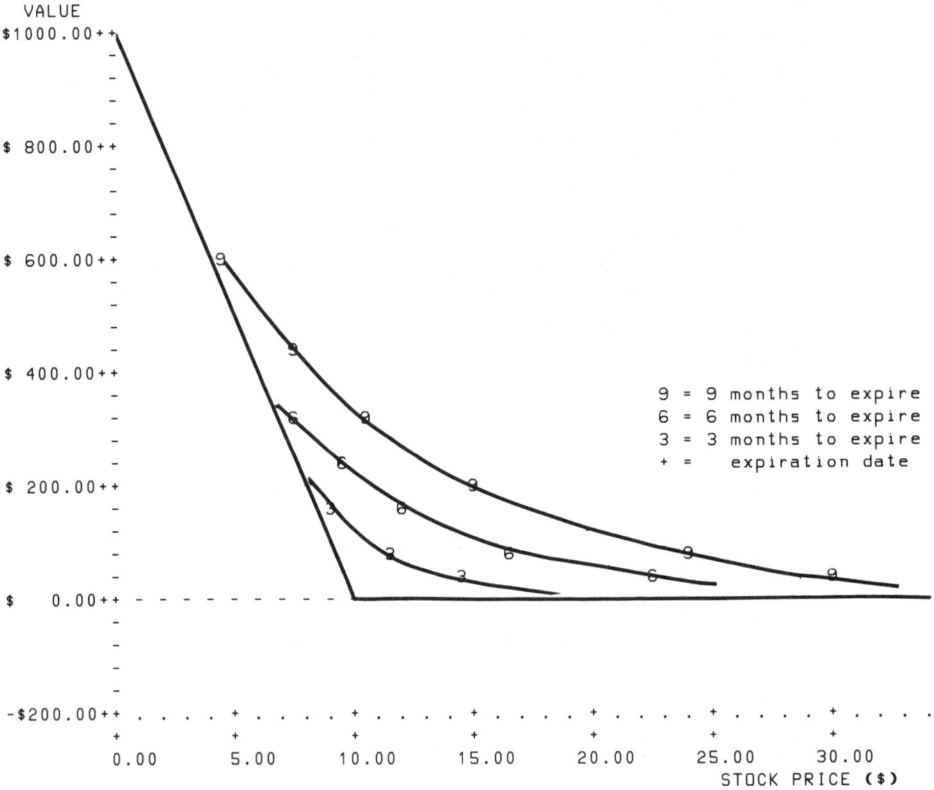

FIGURE 7. FAMILY OF OPTION VALUE CURVES FOR THE PURCHASE OF A PUT OPTION.

TRANSACTION: Buy 1 put option for $100.00 on 100 shares of XYZ company common stock with an exercise price of $10.00 per share.

While the rate of premium reduction is of interest, analysis of the put options can then be restricted to evaluation of the intrinsic or final value curve. The data contained in Table 5 can be displayed pictorially as shown in Figure 8. This graphical representation provides a simple and complete picture of the profitability bounds for the buyer of a put option.

Since every profit made by the buyer is realized as a loss by the seller, it is reasonable to expect that the seller's profit curve will be the inverse of the buyers. This is in fact the case. Figure 9 displays the seller's profit curve. Verification of its mathematical basis is left as an exercise to the reader.

TABLE 5. INTRINSIC VALUE FOR THE PURCHASE OF PUT OPTIONS.

NUMBER OF SHARES	ASSUMED STOCK PRICE	INTRINSIC VALUE (FINAL VALUE)	PROFIT
100	$ 1.00	$ 900.00	$800.00
100	$ 3.00	$ 700.00	$600.00
100	$ 5.00	$ 500.00	$400.00
100	$ 7.00	$ 300.00	$200.00
100	$ 9.00	$ 100.00	$ 0.00
100	$11.00	$ 0.00	−100.00
100	$13.00	$ 0.00	−100.00
100	$15.00	$ 0.00	−100.00
100	$18.00	$ 0.00	−100.00
100	$21.00	$ 0.00	−100.00

TRANSACTION: Buy 1 put option for $100.00 on 100 shares of XYZ company common stock with an exercise price of $10.00 per share.

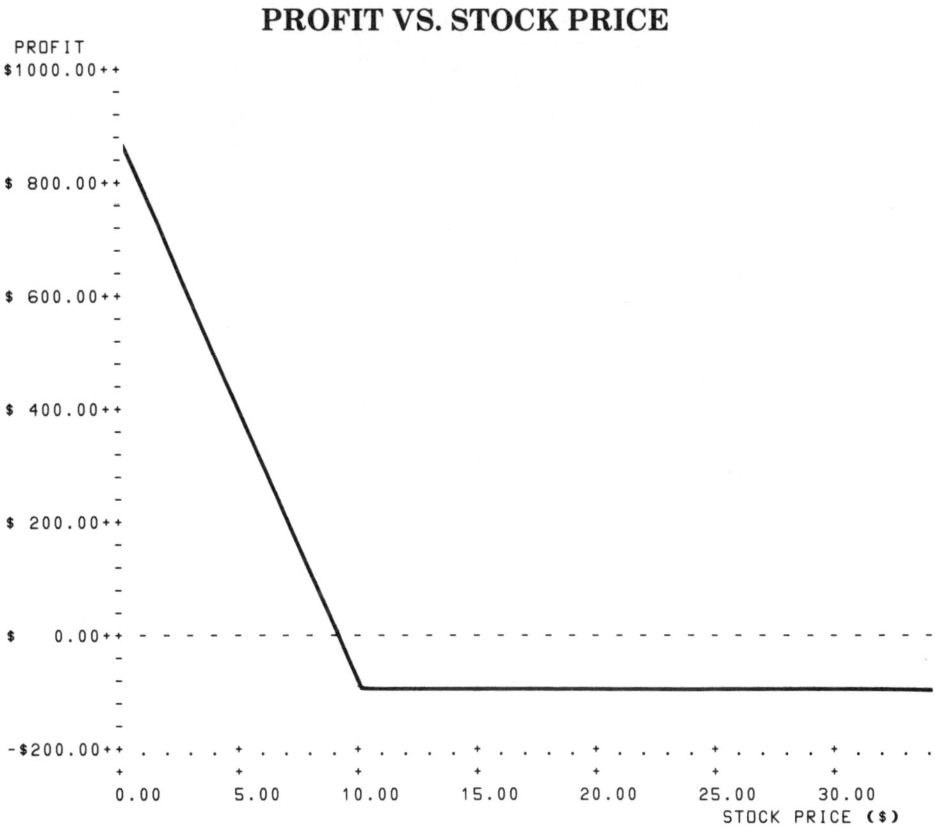

FIGURE 8. PROFIT CURVE FOR THE PURCHASE OF A PUT OPTION EVALUATED AT EXPIRATION.

TRANSACTION: Buy 1 put option for $100.00 on 100 shares of XYZ company common stock with an exercise price of $10.00 per share.

PROFIT VS. STOCK PRICE

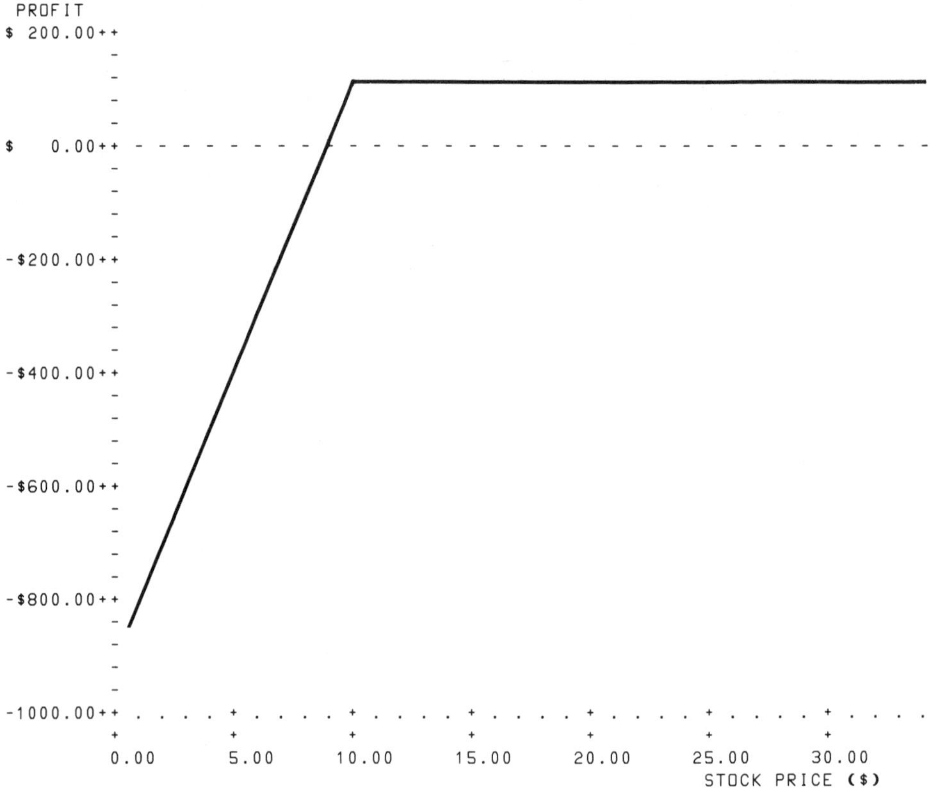

FIGURE 9. PROFIT CURVE FOR THE SHORT SALE OF A PUT OPTION EVALUATED AT EXPIRATION.

TRANSACTION: Sell short 1 put option for $100.00 on 100 shares of XYZ company common stock with an exercise price of $10.00 per share.

2.5 CONVERTIBLE SECURITIES.

Convertible securities provide the investor with a mechanism to participate in a company's potential growth while maintaining a degree of protection during the lean years.

Convertible securities are created to generate capital for the issuing corporation. The conversion privilege allows the corporation to issue these securities to the public at a lower interest rate than possible without the conversion privilege. Once they are on the market however, they offer a unique opportunity for the investor. The convertibles fall into two categories: convertible bonds and convertible preferred stock. As their name indicates, convertible securities are "convertible" into a specified number of shares of common stock at the holders option. In addition to the conversion privilege, these securities typically pay a guaranteed rate of return until maturity. These two features allow the convertible to react with the common stock in an upward market and as a fixed income investment on the down side.

> Consider the example of one XYZ company convertible bond which sells for $1000.00 and is many years from maturity. The Bond is convertible into 50 shares of common stock and has a fixed yield of $100.00 per year.

The conversion value of the bond is the product of the stock price and the conversion ratio. If the stock were to advance to $30.00 per share, the bond, which is convertible into 50 shares, must be worth at least $1500.00. Conversely, if the stock were to fall to $5.00 per share, the bond price would be supported by its fixed income feature of $100.00 per year.

On the down side, the level at which a bond is supported is its investment value. The magnitude of the investment value is a function of the prevailing interest rate and the overall quality of the company of issue. It can be compared to the worth of a bond with the same yield to maturity but without the conversion privilege. Several investment services compute the investment value of convertible securities. These values are generally available through your broker, free of charge.

The conversion value and investment value characteristics of a convertible allow the investor to establish the bounds or asymptotes on the movement of bond price relative to price movement of the underlying common stock. Figure 10 displays the convertible's value curve bounded by its asymptotes. As is the case with options, the convertible's price follows a hyperbolic curve which will approach the asymptotes in the limits. Since convertible securities are rarely held to maturity the hyperbolic curve is of significant interest. Convertibles, like options usually sell for more than their asymptotic limits. This is due to the existence of its fixed income feature at inflated stock prices and its conversion privilege at reduced stock prices. The value of these privileges decreases as they become overshadowed by large conversion values on one hand and low stock price which makes the conversion potential unlikely.

There are several levels of sophistication available when modeling the movement of convertible security prices. The most primitive of these is to simply use the asymptotes and draw a hyperbola through the point defined by the current stock price and current bond price. While this approach is effective, McKean's (Ref 2) Gamma model provides a more precise approximation. Details of this model will be explained in Chapter V.

Translating the convertible's value curve into a profit curve is a simple matter of subtracting the purchase price and adding the yield to each point. Figure 11 displays this result.

In addition to its profit characteristics, convertible securities are senior investment instruments. They generally represent a contractual agreement between the issuer and the holder. As such, they are senior in security to common stock.

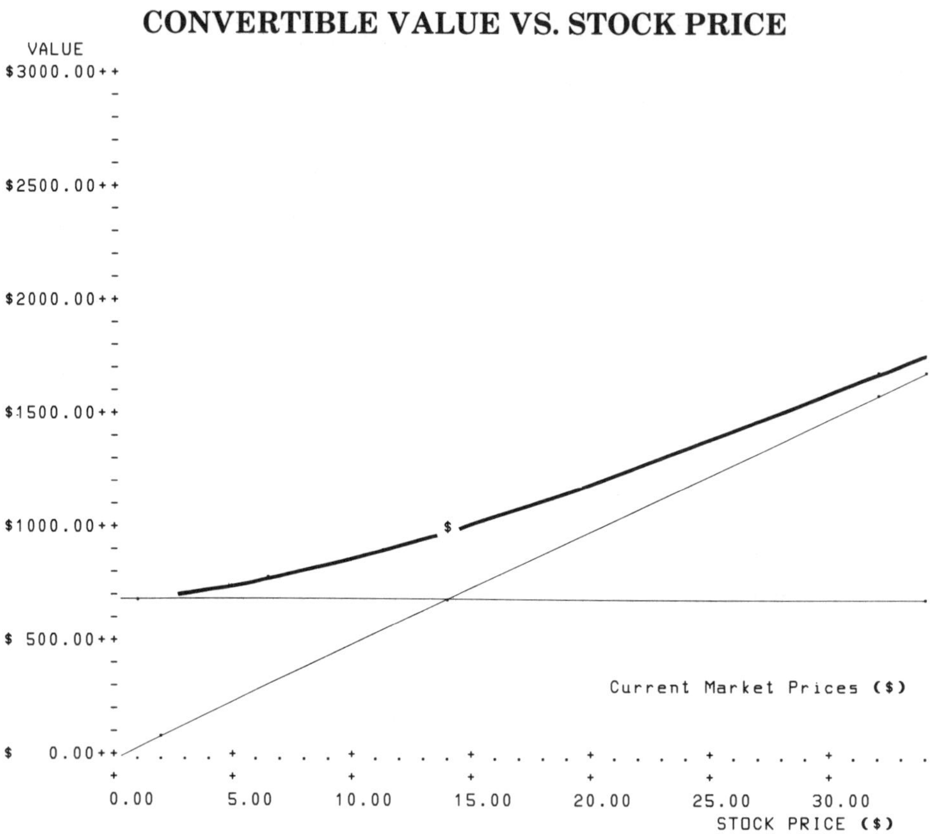

FIGURE 10. CONVERTIBLE SECURITY PRICE AS A FUNCTION OF STOCK PRICE.

TRANSACTION: Buy 1 convertible bond for $1000.00 issued by XYZ company which is convertible into 50 shares of common stock. The bond pays an annual yield of $100.00 per year and has an investment value of $700.00. The current stock price is $14.00 per share.

CONVERTIBLE PROFIT VS. STOCK PRICE

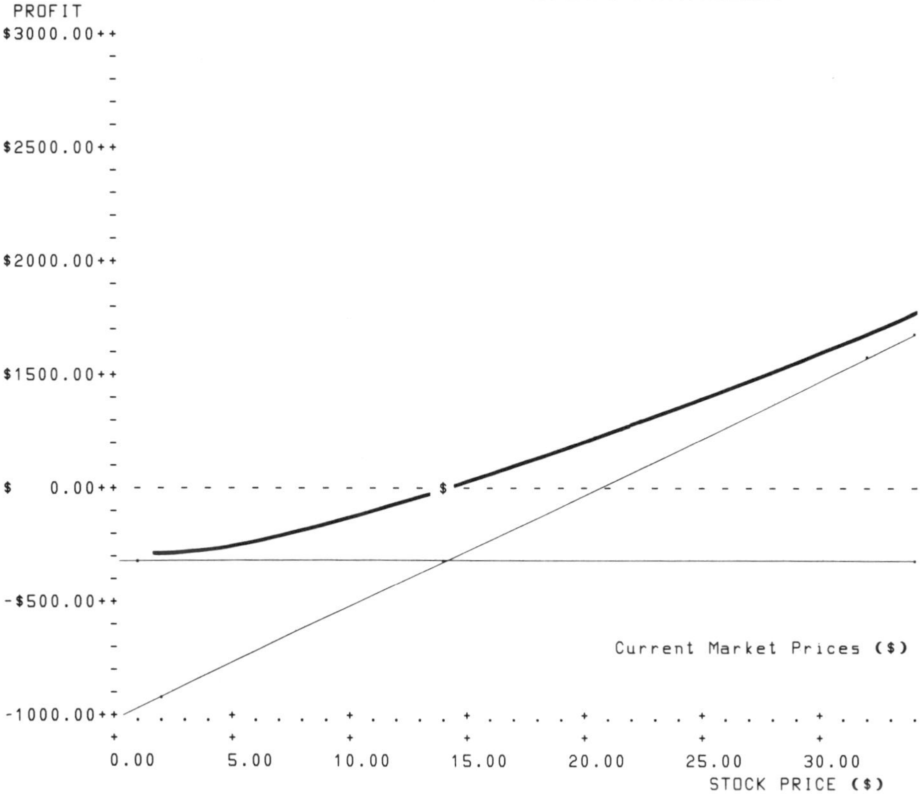

FIGURE 11. PROFIT FROM A CONVERTIBLE SECURITY AS A FUNCTION OF STOCK PRICE.

TRANSACTION: Buy 1 convertible bond for $1000.00 issued by XYZ company which is convertible into 50 shares of common stock. The bond pays a annual yield of $100.00 per year and has an investment value of $700.00. The current stock price is $14.00 per share.

CHAPTER III

THE COMMON DENOMINATOR

3.1 THE ORIGINAL VALUE.

In order to evaluate an investment it is necessary to know what it will cost.

It is simple enough to pay the full price, plus commission, in cash for a security. It is a bit more complicated when the security is purchased on margin. It is complicated further still if the security is sold short. The same problem becomes sporting when both long and short transactions are involved in a single investment position. The problem to which I have been alluding is the "simple" matter of calculating the original value (OV) of the investment. To give this term practical meaning, OV can be defined as the amount of cash which you must take out of your pocket in order to make an investment.

There is one characteristic of this initial cost or OV which can be put forth directly. That is: "OV must represent the total, unbiased cost to enter the position." This includes the commission charges and also any cash equity required by market regulations. It is important to have an honest representation of the total costs.

It may not be obvious to the casual investor why the accuracy of OV is so important. Surely, the amount of profit is of greater concern.

> Consider then an investment in XYZ company which yields a $500.00 profit.

If the original value (OV) of the investment was $1000.00 then the profit is indeed substantial. On the other hand, if the OV was $100,000.00, the investment was hardly worth the effort.

In this example, the profit remained unchanged. However, by using OV as the common denominator the investor can quickly appreciate the worth of his investment.

3.2 COMMISSION CHARGES.

Unless you are a member of the stock exchange, you will pay a commission to transact business through a broker. There are in fact two commission charges which will be incurred. The entry commission, which is charged to purchase the security and the exit commission, which is incurred upon liquidation. If you are truly making an "investment" both the entry and exit commissions must be taken into account.

Evaluation of the quality of an investment, before it is made, is the key to success in the market place. To make a complete assessment it is necessary to quantify the commission costs and factor them into the calculations of OV. Determining the entry commission is a relatively simple matter. The investor need only look up the value in the table which his broker is required, by regulation, to provide. The value of exit commission however, is not as easy to determine in advance. Since commissions are based on the price of the securities at the time of sale, *a priori* determination of exit commission requires a crystal ball.

It is possible to estimate exit commission based on an assumed future stock price, but the investor is still faced with the problem of properly accounting for it. One alternative is to add it to the cost of the initial investment, this approach is unduly conservative. Since exit commission is not paid until liquidation, it can be correctly accounted at that time. Simply subtracting the exit commission from the funds received upon liquidation provides a reasonable and honest accounting for this cost.

> As an example, consider the purchase of 100 shares of XYZ company at $10.00 per share. Entry commission charge is $35.00.

The cost to enter the position (OV) is therefore $1035.00. If the stock is liquidated for $20.00 per share, the net proceeds will be $2000.00, less the commission on the sale. The cost of exit commission in this case is $49.00. Thus the proceeds realized from the sale is $1951.00. The profit on the transaction is the difference between OV ($1035.00) and the net proceeds ($1951.00) which is $916.00 in this example. This method of accounting for exit commission is equally valid when the net result of the transaction is a loss.

Given the same entry conditions as described above, the OV is $1035.00. If the stock is selling for $5.00 per share at liquidation, the commission on 100 shares is $30.00. The proceeds realized at liquidation are therefore $470.00. The net profit from the transaction which is the difference between OV ($1035.00) and the net proceeds ($470.00) is a negative profit (i.e. a loss) of $565.00.

It is important to understand that a loss is also represented as a negative profit. This will allow the mathematics of investing to deal with the broad category of profit with the understanding that losses are not ignored. Stated another way, the profit in the last example is -$565.00.

Since it is important to evaluate exit commissions before an investment is made, the investor has no practical choice but to estimate its magnitude. Given that commissions are directly proportional to stock price, a good first approximation of exit commission is to assume it will equal entry commission. More elaborate schemes of estimation are possible. These may include using the most likely price, a worst case commission value or actually determining the commission for each possible stock price. These methods are left to the discretion of the reader. A careful review of commission schedules will show that estimation improvements provide only small changes in the net proceeds when considered in the light of the magnitude of OV. For the purposes of this text we will assume a constant value of exit commission which is based on the entry commission.

3.3 MARGIN.

To some, margin inherently means high risk; to others, it is a means to play the market for higher stakes. In fact, margin is simply a loan for which the securities are collateral. The amount of down payment, which must be made in order to purchase securities on margin, is set by the Federal Reserve Board. The amount was as low as 10% of the value of the securities in the 1920's. This practice helped fuel the crash of 1929. As stocks dropped, investors on margin were called to provide additional collateral to cover the declining value of the stocks. Since the down turn was large, and over a broad range of stocks, it took only a few weeks for entire portfolios to be wiped out. In 1984, the margin rate stands at 50%. In order to buy securities on margin, the investor is allowed to borrow up to 50% of the value of the securities. Once the securities are purchased however, a second rate, called maintenance margin, is applied. Typically, maintenance margin requires less capital then entry margin. This provides a pad against price fluctuations after the securities are purchased. In 1984, with entry margin set at 50%, the maintenance margin was set at 30%. Stated another way, the investor is required to maintain an equity of 30% of the value of the securities on margin. If the stock price falls to a level such that the equity is less than 30% of the security value, a margin call occurs. The investor is required to provide additional capital or securities to increase his account equity back to the 50% threshold.

As with any loan, the investor is required to pay interest on the amount borrowed. The rate is tied to the short term prime interest rate. Based on the amount of the debit balance, up to 2 percentage points over prime rate or broker call rate is charged. The investor with a small debit balance, typically below $10,000.00, will be required to pay the prime rate plus 2%. As the debit balance increases, the delta interest rate charged over prime rate decreases. In effect, large borrowers get a volume discount to buy securities on margin. Your brokerage firm will provide the rate structure upon request.

Margin calculations are performed on the total account. However, not all securities are marginable. Those securities that are not marginable are excluded from the equity calculations on which the margin computation is made. Generally, lower quality stocks are not marginable. Your broker can tell you if a specific security falls in this category.

3.4 ACCOUNTING FOR MARGIN INTEREST.

If the investor chooses to purchase securities on margin, the interest on the debit balance created is a valid, accountable charge to the investment. Since interest rates historically fluctuate over a narrow band and the debit balance fluctuates with the security price, the assumption that the margin interest charges will remain unchanged over the period of the investment is the only reasonable option to estimate this cost.

Using the average value approach to determine the magnitude of the interest charges does not completely resolve the problem of accounting for margin interest. It still remains to define "when" to account for the interest charges. In actuality, interest is charged daily over the duration of the investment. Accounting for interest charges on this basis is a tedious task which results in only fractional differences in the profit when compared to an end loaded method.

Use of the end loading simply means accounting for the interest cost at entry by adding it to OV, or at liquidation by subtracting it from the net proceeds. Both approaches are inherently imprecise but the error introduced is acceptably small. Accounting for interest charges at entry is the more conservative of the two approaches, but also the furthest from the truth. Since there is a difference between entry and maintenance margin the cost can actually be deferred until liquidation. In effect, the interest is deducted from the 50% cash equity required at entry into the investment. Interest charges generally range from 1% to 2% of this equity per month. Since only 30% equity is required by maintenance margin, and 50% equity is present initially, the reduction in equity caused by interest charges is not significant. Based on these considerations, margin interest can be accurately accounted when the position is liquidated along with the exit commission.

3.5 COMPUTING OV.

Since we have explored the merits of an honest assessment of the investment cost, the task remains to compute OV and to estimate the exit commission and margin interest charges.

As presented in Chapter II there are four basic security types. If these four types are available for a single company, the presence of more than one in an investment account may alter the calculation of OV. In addition, three of the four types can be profitably bought or sold short. The result is effectively seven basic investment instruments. In the interest of clarity, the seven investment instruments are restated from Chapter II.

1. Long the Common Stock.
2. Long the Convertible Security.
3. Long the Put Option.
4. Long the Call Option.
5. Short the Common Stock.
6. Short the Call Option.
7. Short the Put Option.

In dealing with these instruments to compute OV, let us begin with the simplest case and work towards the most complex.

3.5.1 LONG THE COMMON STOCK.

To compute OV for the purchase of common stock, the simplest of rules are applied. Entry commission can be determined from a table supplied by your broker. The cost of the securities is the product of the number of shares times the price. OV then is the sum of this cost and the entry commission. This case is termed, "the 100% margin case" since 100% of the required cash is paid.

To compute OV for the case where margin is employed, multiply the 100% margin cost by the entry margin rate. This new figure plus the entry commission represents the OV on margin. The debit balance (DB) which is generated is the difference between the full cash OV (OV_{100}) minus the OV computed on margin (OV_{50}).

The computation for OV can be stated concisely using an equation as the mathematical representation of the process. In short then:

$$OV_M = (N * S * M) + C_e \qquad \text{(Eq 3-1)}$$

Where: OV_M = Original Value for the Margin Rate.

N = Number of Securities.

S = Security Price.

M = Margin Factor (as a decimal fraction of 1.0).

C_e = Entry Commission.

The debit balance calculation can be similarly stated:

$$DB = OV_{100} - OV_{50} \qquad \text{(Eq 3-2)}$$

Where: DB = Debit Balance.

OV_{100} = Original Value on 100% Margin.

OV_{50} = Original Value on 50% Margin.

To apply these equations;

> Consider the purchase of 100 shares of XYZ company common stock for $12.00 per share with an entry commission of $37.80.

Applying equation 3-1, we have:

$$OV_{100} = (100 * \$12.00 * 1.00) + \$37.80$$

$$OV_{100} = \$1237.80$$

and

$$OV_{50} = (100 * \$12.00 * .50) + \$37.80$$

$$OV_{50} = \$637.80$$

and applying equation 3-2;

$$DB = \$1237.80 - \$637.80$$

$$DB = \$600.00$$

In this case of the purchase of common stock the equation for OV and DB are applied by inserting the appropriate values and "turning the crank." In a few simple steps with your hand calculator, out pops the solution. To the uninitiated, mathematical representations might look foreboding. The reader is encouraged to put aside any apprehension and work with these equations. In short order, you will find that the equations are easier to follow than the same statements in written text.

3.5.2 LONG THE CONVERTIBLE SECURITY.

The purchase of convertible securities is handled in the same manner as the purchase of common stock. Both equations 3-1 and 3-2 are applied directly to compute the original value (OV) and the debit balance (DB). There is, in addition, another quantity which will be of interest. Since convertible securities are distinctive because of their conversion privilege, it is sometimes necessary to know the equivalent shares (ES) of common stock of an investment in convertible securities. To determine ES, the following equation is applied:

$$ES = N * CR \qquad \text{(Eq 3-3)}$$

Where: ES = Equivalent Number of Shares.

N = Number of Convertible Securities.

CR = Conversion Ratio.

The application of ES will be explained later in this chapter. The reader is encouraged to work some problems to compute OV, DB, and ES until he feels comfortable with the application of these equations.

3.5.3 LONG THE PUT OR CALL OPTION.

The purchase of both put and call options can only be accomplished on 100% margin. The investor must pay the full cash price when purchasing options. OV is computed using equation 3-1 while applying the 100% margin factor. Since margin cannot be used, the debit balance calculation is not applicable to option purchases. Options are written on 100 share blocks of common stock. The equivalent shares (ES) calculation is simply 100 times the number of options involved.

3.5.4 SHORT THE COMMON STOCK.

If the investment involves a short sale of common stock, the investor is, in effect, borrowing and selling the stock of another investor. Since there is a defacto loan, the short investor is required to post collateral. The amount of collateral is a function of the entry margin rate and the net short position. In the case of a naked short sale, the only capital the seller must provide is this collateral. The amount of collateral is described by the equation:

$$C_{post} = N * S * M \qquad \text{(Eq 3-4)}$$

Where: C_{post} = Collateral to be Posted.

N = Number of Securities Sold Short

S = Security Price.

M = Margin Rate (as a decimal fraction of 1.0).

Since only commissions are required in addition to C_{post}, the equation for OV for the short sale of stock is the sum of C_{post} and entry commission.

$$OV = C_{post} + C_e \qquad \text{(Eq 3-5)}$$

Where: OV = Original Value.

C_{post} = Collateral to be Posted.

C_e = Entry Commission.

When a stock is sold short, a credit is posted in the sellers account. The investor is prohibited from drawing on this balance. In addition, he is required to maintain an account equity (C_{post}), which is described by equation 3-4. As was previously the case, the entry margin factor is used initially and the maintenance margin factor is applied once the position is established. While this equity can be in the form of cash, it is also possible to use marginable securities to serve as the collateral. Since no monies are actually borrowed, debit balance calculations are not applicable to a short sale.

> Consider the example in which an investor sells short 100 shares of XYZ company common stock at \$12.00 per share. The entry commission from the tables is \$37.80.

The proceeds from the sale are credited to the investors account. In addition, the investor is required to post collateral for the short sale. Applying equations 3-4 and 3-5:

$$C_{post} = 100 * \$12.00 * .50$$

$$C_{post} = \$600.00$$

and

$$OV = \$600.00 + \$37.80$$

$$OV = \$637.80$$

There is an interesting twist when dealing in short sales. It is possible for an investor to hold an equivalent long position in convertible securities while he is short the common stock. This situation occurs when the investor owns convertible securities which are convertible into the shorted common. If the investor's equivalent long position is greater than or equal to the short position, no collateral is required for the short sale.

As a general rule in compound investment situations, the OV calculation is the sum of the individual OV's of the component securities. Caution must be exercised however to insure that the proper security relationships, such as the collateral in this case, are observed.

> Let us assume that an investor buys 3 XYZ convertible bonds for $1000.00. The bonds are convertible into 40.5 shares of common stock. In addition, the investor also sells short 100 shares of XYZ common stock for $17.00 per share. The total entry commission from the tables is $67.80.

To solve for OV we must first compute the equivalent shares using equation 3-3.

$$ES = 3 * 40.5$$

$$ES = 121.5 \text{ shares}$$

Since ES is greater than the short position (100 shares) no additional equity is required by the short sale. Using equations 3-1 and 3-2 to compute OV we have:

$$OV_{100} = (3 * \$1000.00 * 1.00) + \$67.80$$

$$OV_{100} = \$3067.80$$

and

$$OV_{50} = (3 * \$1000.00 * .50) + \$67.80$$

$$OV_{50} = \$1567.80$$

and

$$DB = \$3067.80 - \$1567.80$$

$$DB = \$1500.00$$

The problem becomes a bit more sporting when the short position exceeds the equivalent long position. There is interaction between the cash collateral for the short sale and any debit balance which might be generated from the use of margin. In effect, the cash collateral serves a double duty as both collateral for the short and to reduce the debit balance for the long position which is on margin.

3.5.5 SYNERGISTIC EFFECTS ON OV.

In compound investment situations, it is possible to post securities in lieu of cash to satisfy any collateral (C_{post}) requirements. This feature affects the OV_{100} calculation for the investment by reducing or eliminating the amount of C_{post} required. Long securities which have been paid for in full have a collateral value which is tied to margin rate. This collateral value (C_{val}) can be determined using:

$$C_{val} = (1.0 - M) * N * S \qquad \text{(Eq 3-6)}$$

Where: C_{val} = Collateral Value of the Long Securities.

M = Margin Factor (as a decimal fraction of 1.0).

N = Number of Securities.

S = Security Price.

If C_{val} is greater than C_{post} then C_{post} can be set to zero for the OV_{100} calculation. If C_{val} is less than C_{post} then the difference between these values must be posted in cash.

This process has one additional twist. If you add another unrelated security to your account, its collateral value can also be applied to reduce the C_{post} requirements for the OV_{100} calculation. The reader is cautioned that this feature applies only to marginable securities which are held in an account whose equity exceeds the entry margin requirements. As a rule of thumb, if your account has more equity than entry margin requires, this equity can be applied to reduce the C_{post} requirement for the next investment situation.

Consider the purchase of 5 XYZ company convertible bonds for $1200.00 each. The conversion ratio of the bond is 50 shares of

> common stock. In addition, the investor sells short 350 shares of XYZ company common stock for \$20.00 per share. The total entry commission is \$118.00.

To begin the problem we must first determine the number of equivalent shares which the bonds represent. Applying equation 3-3 then:

$$ES = 5 * 50$$

$$ES = 250 \text{ shares}$$

Since the short sale involves 350 shares, we have a net short position of 100 shares. The collateral required can be computed using equation 3-4 for the net short shares.

$$C_{post} = 100 * \$20.00 * .50$$

$$C_{post} = \$1000.00$$

The collateral value of the long security can be computed using equation 3-6.

$$C_{val} = (1.0 - 0.50) * 5 * 1200.00$$

$$C_{val} = \$3000.00$$

Since C_{val} is greater than C_{post} there is no collateral required (C_{post} = \$0.00) for the OV_{100} calculation.

$$OV_{100} = (5 * \$1200.00 * 1.00) + \$0.00 + \$118.00$$

$$OV_{100} = \$6118.00$$

However, collateral is required if the transaction is done on 50% margin.

$$OV_{50} = (5 * \$1200.00 * .50) + \$1000.00 + \$118.00$$

$$OV_{50} = \$4118.00$$

The debit balance calculation is:

$$DB = \$6118.00 - \$4118.00$$

$$DB = \$2000.00$$

The affect of the synergism between the long and short securities is a reduction in the cash required in the 100% margin case or a reduction in the debit balance in the 50% margin case. This reduction is permitted because, in effect, the investor has posted the long securities as collateral and their value exceeds the collateral requirements for the short position.

3.5.6 SHORT THE CALL OPTION.

The investor who sells a call option is in fact selling a contract through which he promises to deliver, upon demand, 100 shares of a specified common stock at a specified price. There is no loan of securities as is the case with the short sale of common stock. However, the option contract must be secured. There are two methods to provide this security. The first is to use 100 shares of the common stock or an equivalent holding in convertible securities. In this case the option is considered covered. Alternately, cash collateral or marginable securities can be posted. Unlike the short sale of common stock, the proceeds of the option sale are immediately available to the seller. They can be applied as part of the cash collateral or withdrawn from the account.

The computation of OV for the sale of call options is dependent upon their covered or uncovered status. In either case however, the first step is to determine the cash credit for the sale.

$$C_c = N * O_p \qquad \text{(Eq 3-7)}$$

Where: C_c = Cash Credit.

N = Number of Options.

O_p = Option price.

For all uncovered options, the investor must post collateral. The amount is determined by applying the following equation:

$$C_{post} = N*(MAX(100*((1.3*S)-E)) \text{ or } (\$250.00)) \qquad \text{(Eq 3-8)}$$

Where: C_{post} = Cash Collateral to be Posted.

N = Number of Options.

S = Common Stock Price.

E = Exercise Price of the Option.

The MAX function requires the investor to select the larger between the computed value and $250.00. OV for the sale of uncovered options can be described by the equation:

$$OV = C_{post} - C_c + C_e \qquad \text{(Eq 3-9)}$$

Where: OV = Original Value.

C_{post} = Collateral to be Posted.

C_c = Cash Credit from Option Sale.

C_e = Entry Commission.

To understand this investment, let us work the following example:

> Consider the short sale of 2 options for \$150.00 each on 100 shares of XYZ company common stock. The current price of XYZ common is \$14.00 and the exercise price of the option is \$15.00. The entry commission is \$32.50.

In solving for OV the investor must first compute the cash credit using equation 3-7.

$$C_c = 2 * \$150.00$$

$$C_c = \$300.00$$

Next the collateral to be posted must be determined. This is accomplished by applying equation 3-8.

$$C_{post} = 2 *(MAX(100*((1.3*\$14.00)-\$15.00))or(\$250.00))$$

$$C_{post} = 2 *(MAX(\$320.00 \text{ or } \$250.00))$$

$$C_{post} = \$640.00$$

Finally, applying equation 3-9, OV can be determined.

$$OV = \$640.00 - \$300.00 + \$32.50$$

$$OV = \$372.50$$

In short then, the investor must pay \$372.50 in order to sell these two uncovered call options.

Covered call options do not require the investor to post collateral. The covered condition is determined by computing the equivalent long position of the common stock and applying those shares to the number of shares under the option contract. Since option contracts have been standardized, the number of shares under contract is 100 times the number of options. To determine the number of options that can be covered by an equivalent number of common shares, equation 3-10 is applied.

$$N_c = \text{MOD}(\ ES\ /\ 100\ ) \qquad \text{(Eq 3-10)}$$

Where: N_c = Number of Covered Options.

ES = Equivalent Shares Long.

The MOD function causes the result of the division to be rounded off by dropping any decimal fraction.

It is to the investor's advantage, if multiple options are involved, to use the equivalent shares to cover the most expensive options (i.e. the options which require the largest C_{post}) thus reducing the overall magnitude of OV.

In addition to using common stock or equivalent shares to cover an option, it is possible to purchase and use another call option. An investment of this type is called a spread. OV calculations of spreads are not particularly germane to this thesis but are adequately covered by Gastineau in appendix A of Reference 3.

> Consider the example of an investor who holds 5 convertible bonds each convertible into 50 shares of common stock.

Applying equation 3-3, we have:

$$ES = 5 * 50$$

$$ES = 250 \text{ shares.}$$

Next, applying equation 3-10 to determine the number of options which can be covered we have:

$$N_c = \text{MOD}(\ 250\ /\ 100\ )$$

$$N_c = \text{MOD}(\ 2.50\ )$$

$$N_c = 2$$

The number of covered options which can be written is two. Options which are only partially covered are treated as uncovered options. Computing OV for the combination of covered and uncovered options, in a single transaction, is similar to the example involving the short sale of stock described in the preceding section.

> Consider the purchase of 5 XYZ company convertible bonds for $1200.00 each. The bond is convertible into 30 shares. In addition, sell 2 call options on XYZ company for $300.00 each with an exercise price of $40.00. The current stock price is $35.00 and the entry commission is $85.00.

Let us begin this problem by determining the cash credit from the sale of the options. Using equation 3-7 we have;

$$C_c = 2 * \$300.00$$

$$C_c = \$600.00$$

To determine the equivalent share we must apply equation 3-3.

$$Es = 5 * 30$$

$$Es = 150 \text{ shares}$$

Next, applying equation 3-10 we have;

$$N_c = MOD\ (150/100)$$

$$N_c = MOD\ (1.5)$$

$$N_c = 1$$

To determine the collateral to be posted for the one uncovered option we apply equation 3-8.

$$C_{post} = 1*(MAX(100*((1.3*\$35)-\$40) \text{ or } \$250))$$

$$C_{post} = 1*(MAX(\$550 \text{ or } \$250))$$

$$C_{post} = \$550.00$$

Next, we determine the collateral value of the long securities, in this case 5 convertible bonds;

$$C_{val} = (1.0-0.50) * 5 * \$1200.00$$

$$C_{val} = 0.50 * \$6000.00$$

$$C_{val} = \$3000.00$$

Since C_{val} is greater than C_{post}, no additional collateral is required for the OV_{100} calculation. Combining the OV_{100} equation 3-1 for the convertible and the OV equation 3-8 for the option we have;

$$OV_{100} = (5 * \$1200 * 1.00) + \$0.00 - \$600 + \$85$$

$$OV_{100} = \$5485.00$$

and

$$OV_{50} = (5 * \$1200 * 0.50) + \$550 - \$600 + \$85$$

$$OV_{50} = \$3035.00$$

and

$$DB = \$5485.00 - \$3035.00$$

$$DB = \$2450.00$$

Thank heavens! We seem to have reached the bottom line. All that just to determine how much to take out of your pocket for this investment. Perhaps its time to lynch the accountant who made this process so complicated. Unfortunately, while a lynch party might make us all feel good, the system probably wouldn't change anyway. If you work a few examples on your own you might decide that it's not so bad after all.

3.5.7 SHORT THE PUT OPTION.

Computing OV for the put option is similar to the OV calculation for the call option. As with call writing, the proceeds from the sale of puts are immediately available to the seller. The cash credit for put writing, like call writing, is described by equation 3-7. The cash credit is the product of the number of puts and the put price. The determination of collateral to be posted (C_{post}) is best described using the specialized formula of equation 3-11.

$$C_{post} = N*(MAX(100*(E-.7*S)) \text{ or } (\$250.00)) \qquad \text{(Eq 3-11)}$$

Where: C_{post} = Collateral to be Posted.

N = Number of Puts.

E = Exercise Price.

S = Stock Price.

Once the collateral is determined, the actual computation of OV for put writing is described by equation 3-9 and is therefore the same as for call writing.

> Consider the example of an investor who writes 3 put options for $450.00 each on 100 shares of XYZ company common stock. The exercise price of the put is $15.00. The common stock price at the time of the transaction is $12.00. The total entry commission is $52.31.

Applying equation 3-7 to compute the cash credit:

$$C_c = 3 * \$450.00$$

$$C_c = \$1350.00$$

The collateral to be posted is determined using equation 3-11.

$$C_{post} = 3 * (MAX(100*(\$15-(.7*\$12)) \text{ or } (\$250))$$

$$C_{post} = 3 * (MAX(\$660 \text{ or } \$250))$$

$$C_{post} = \$1980.00$$

Finally, by applying equation 3-9, OV can be determined.

$$OV = \$1980.00 - \$1350.00 + \$52.31$$

$$OV = \$682.31$$

The issue of covered put writing is one which is surrounded by some controversy. Theoretically, a short position in common stock should provide coverage for the put writer. Since a loss on the put can only occur when the stock declines, this would be offset by a corresponding gain on the short position. The Option Clearing Corporation holds that put options can not be covered by a short position in the common stock. Because of this, the Clearing Corporation requires its member firms to post collateral to cover put writing. This requirement is passed along by the brokerage firms to their investors.

As is the case with call writing, put options can be covered in spread situations by purchasing like put options. The rules which govern the computation of OV are covered in detail in Appendix A of Gastineau's book (Ref 3).

3.6 ACCOUNT WIDE COMPUTATIONS.

As the investor enters a number of investment situations, his brokerage account will grow. As this occurs, an equity relationship will develop between the various securities in his portfolio. Accounting for an investor's holding is standardized throughout the industry. This standardization however, is sometimes limited to sub-account balances and does not include the overall equity value of the portfolio. On a total account basis, the investor is primarily concerned with his net worth, or equity, and his debit balance. Some brokerage firms compute these parameters and provide them to the investor with his monthly statement and others do not. In either case, it is useful for the investor to understand the mathematical process of these account wide computations.

An investor's account is divided into several sub-accounts. When an investment is entered, the transaction of the component securities are carried out in appropriate sub-accounts. The treatment of these sub-accounts as dependent portions of the total account supports the situation dependent computation of OV, which was presented earlier in this chapter. These sub-account categories are enumerated below.

TYPE	DESCRIPTION
0.	Non-Conv. Debt Securities Margin.
1.	Cash.
2.	General Margin.
3.	Short.
4.	Dividend and Interest Income.
5.	When Issued Margin Trades.
6.	Government Securities Margin Account.
7.	(Not Used).
8.	Special Subscription.
9.	Convertible Debt Securities.

Each of these sub-accounts will have its own balance and the sum of these is the overall account balance. In order to compute the equity for the account, the following equation is applied.

$$EQ = SUM(V_L) - SUM(Vs) + A_{bal} \qquad \text{(Eq 3-12)}$$

Where: EQ = Equity or Investors Net Worth

V_L = Value of the Long Securities.

V_S = Value of the Short Securities.

A_{bal} = Overall Account Balance.

The SUM function is simply the addition of the values of all elements which fall in the stated class (i.e. V_L). In order to compute the debit balance for the account, equation 3-13 is applied.

$$DB_{ac} = A_{bal} - SUM(V_3) \qquad \text{(Eq 3-13)}$$

Where: DB_{ac} = Debit Balance for the Account.

A_{bal} = Overall Account Balance.

V_3 = Value of the Short Securities in the Type 3 Account.

On a regular basis equity in the account is recomputed. Through this process, the brokerage firm also recomputes the account wide debit balance and makes the appropriate interest charges to the account. As prices fluctuate, paper transfers are made between the sub-accounts. These transactions are, for all practical purposes, transparent to the investor. It should be noted that small discrepancies may exist between the brokerage firm's computation and those performed by the investor. These usually can be attributed to the differences in the securities prices used in the respective computation. Any large discrepancies should be explored. Generally, the error will be due to some special situation which the investor did not account for properly.

There are some additional account wide parameters of interest. These include the amount available for borrowing (margin) and the current interest rate. These parameters vary from day to day and are best determined by a call to your broker. They are usually available at his fingertips and are not subject to negotiation.

CHAPTER IV

THE STANDARD OF MEASURE

4.1 APPLES AND ORANGES.

The only goal of any investment is to realize a profit. This statement must underlie all investment decisions. There is then a need for comparison both within the microcosm of investment situations and within the macrocosm of all possible financial opportunities. The basis for this comparison between investments must be rooted in profit potential. There is however a pitfall which must be avoided. It was in grade school that we learned that one must not add apples and oranges. With this in mind, it is necessary for the investor to choose a standard of measure for the comparison which can be applied to any investment opportunity.

The first choice for this standard of measure might be the profit itself, expressed in dollars. This method alone does not provide an unbiased measure of the investment's potential. Other important considerations include both time and the original value (OV) of the investment.

> Consider an investment of $1000.00 in two different situations. Situation "A" yields a profit of $30.00 in 26 weeks while situation "B" yields a profit of $50.00 in 52 weeks.

At first glance, the $50.00 yield of situation "B" may look more profitable, a closer examination however, will reveal that the $30.00 profit of situation "A" is a superior return. The important difference between these two cases, since OV is a constant $1,000.00, is the time factor. Situation "A" yields $30.00 in half the time of situation "B". Theoretically, the investor will be able to reinvest his capital after the 26 weeks of situation "A" with similar results. Ignoring the potential for compounding, the return from situation "A" can be projected to be $60.00 for 52 weeks.

4.2 ANNUALIZED PERCENT PROFIT.

The banking industry has long realized the necessity of including time and OV in its profitability statements. The use of interest rates expressed in percent, accounts for the time factor and is independent of OV. This percentage, however, is complicated by variations in the period after which the interest is realized. In addition, interest left on deposit will compound by drawing interest in the next period. The myriad of interest rates and compounding periods creates some confusion when choosing between the various banking institutions. A single, consistent standard is necessary. The banking community's defacto standard is effective annual rate of return.

The solution to this dilemma for the investor is to select a standard of measure which is compatible with both the banking community and his investment analysis. The standard of measure which meets this criteria is the same as for the banking community. That is; the expression of profits in terms of their effective annualized interest rate. This will standardize both the time and OV variations between different investments and also permit easy comparison to the banking community.

Applying the annualized percent profit approach to the previous example the relative quality of the choice is clear. Using simple interest as the standard of measure, the effective annualized rate for situation "A" is 6% while the rate for situation "B" is 5%. Clearly then, situation "A" is a more profitable investment.

In the final analysis, the comparison between investments must be expanded to include the terms which are readily available through other institutions. The 6% return from situation "A" may not be superior to the rate of return of a neighborhood bank. Since profit is the investor's ultimate objective, there is no reason to invest in securities if a greater profit can be achieved, risk free, from another source.

The banking community offers many and varied interest rates to the investor. These are based on the amount of capital invested, and other restrictions on the liquidity of the investment. Generally, bank interest rates are defined as an annualized percentage with some level of compounding. The level of compounding has a significant effect on the profits, and rates may be quoted as simple interest through compounding every instant. The effect of changes in compounding can best be described through use of a sample investment.

> Consider then, an investment of $10,000.00, at 15% interest, left on deposit for a period of 1 year.

The variations in the profit for this investment, as a function of changes in compounding, are displayed in Table 6. The difference in return between simple annualized interest and interest compounded every instant is over 1% of the original value. A careful review of this data, however, will also show that the delta in the profit grows smaller for each incremental change in compounding. The difference between weekly compounding and compounding every second is hardly worth serious consideration in a comparative measurement.

The effective annualized interest measure provides a common basis to judge both the banking community and security investments. As such, it meets our requirements as a standard of measure. In its effective annualized form, %P is computed as a percentage of the ratio of final value (FVI) and original value (OV) and projected for one year. The equation which defines this process is described below.

TABLE 6. PROFIT AS A FUNCTION OF COMPOUNDING.

COMPOUNDING	ORIGINAL VALUE	FINAL VALUE	PROFIT	EFFECTIVE ANNUAL RATE
ANNUALLY	$10,000.00	$11,500.00	$1,500.00	15.00%
SEMI – ANNUALLY	$10,000.00	$11,556.25	$1,556.25	15.56%
QUARTERLY	$10,000.00	$11,586.50	$1,586.50	15.87%
WEEKLY	$10,000.00	$11,615.83	$1,615.83	16.16%
DAILY	$10,000.00	$11,617.99	$1,617.99	16.18%
INSTANTLY	$10,000.00	$11,618.17	$1,618.17	16.18%

TRANSACTION: Deposit $10,000.00 for 52 weeks in a 15% savings account.

$$\%P = 100 * ((FVI / OV) - 1) / T \qquad \text{(Eq 4-1)}$$

$$\%P = \frac{100}{T} * \left[\frac{FVI}{OV} - 1\right]$$

Where: %P = Percent Profit with Effective Annualized Interest.

FVI = Final Value of the Investment.

OV = Original Value of the Investment.

T = Time of the Investment (in years).

To apply this equation, let us;

> Consider the example of an investor who purchases 100 shares of XYZ company at \$10.00 per share with an annual dividend of \$0.12 per share. The entry commission is \$30.00 and the intended holding period is 43 weeks.

To compute the effective annualized percent profit, the investor must first select a final stock price. For this example, let us select a final stock price of \$12.00 per share. It follows that, the exit commission for the investment is \$31.79. The dividend received for the investment will be estimated by using the fractional portion of the total dividend for the holding period. The final value of the investment can be computed using the technique described in Chapter II for the purchase of common stock. The FVI is simply the product of the number of shares purchased, times the value of each share, less any commission charges. Stated in more common terms, the final value of an investment is the cash you put back into your pocket when the investment is liquidated. In this case, the value of the shares is the estimated \$12.00 market value, plus the accrued dividend.

$$FVI = 100 * (\$12.00 + (\$.12 * 43/52)) - \$31.79$$

$$FVI = \$1178.13$$

The original value is determined using equation 3-1 for the 100% margin case.

$$OV_{100} = (100 * \$10.00 * 1.00) + 30.00$$

$$OV_{100} = \$1030.00$$

Applying the effective annualized interest equation 4-1 we have:

$$\%P = 100 * ((1178.13/1030.00) - 1)/(43/52)$$

$$\%P = 100 * (0.1438) / (0.8269)$$

$$\%P = 17.4\%$$

As a standard of measure, effective annualized percent profit implies that compounding will occur at the conclusion of the security's holding period. The realities of the market place, notably commission considerations, penalize the investor through increased cost to take small profits frequently. This more than offsets any gain that might be available through compounding. The purist would insist that the use of effective annualized percent profit errs slightly in the favor of conservatism. For the average investor, this is an acceptable situation.

4.3 HOW MUCH IS ENOUGH?

In all of us there is a desire to get rich quick. Admittedly, it would be nice to parlay a $1.00 investment into $1,000,000.00 over night. Unfortunately, for every million dollar winner in the lottery, there are literally millions of gamblers who threw their dollar down the proverbial hole. In cold harsh terms, if you can simply double your investment you have achieved a significant accomplishment. The catch here is the time factor.

Your neighborhood bank will double your investment, risk free. At 5.9%, compounded annually, a bank will double your equity in a mere 12 years. This may not be impressive however. So, armed with your Wall Street Journal and visions of grandeur, you enter the stock market.

As any experienced investor will attest, it is tough to win all the time. Big wins come with big risks, and sometimes big losses. A question which each investor must answer is: "How much is enough?" If you have been an investor, it might prove both interesting and sobering to compute your own performance in terms of annualized percent profit. The performance available from a bank is a good starting point for any comparison. Another benchmark is the long term performance of the professionally managed mutual funds. This exercise might well result in an appreciation of a sustained profit rate which is as little as 15%. Admittedly, this is not an earth shaking figure but in the light of a lifetime it will prove to be significant. If thrills and chills are a prime objective, long term return is probably not important. Whatever the basis, only the individual investor can decide how much is enough.

To correlate the goal to double the investment in terms of percent profit and time, Table 7 is provided. At the low end of the scale are the effective annual rates offered by the banking community. As you approach the higher values of %P the time to double equity decreases. At 26% compounded annually, for example, equity will double in just under 3 years. As we move toward the high end of the %P scale, equal changes in %P result in ever smaller reductions in the time to double equity.

TABLE 7. TIME TO DOUBLE EQUITY.

PERCENT PROFIT	TIME
2%	35.00 years
4%	17.67 years
6%	11.89 years
8%	9.00 years
10%	7.27 years
12%	6.12 years
14%	5.29 years
16%	4.67 years
18%	4.18 years
20%	3.80 years
22%	3.48 years
24%	3.22 years
26%	3.00 years
28%	2.81 years
30%	2.64 years
32%	2.50 years
34%	2.37 years
36%	2.25 years
38%	2.15 years
40%	2.06 years
50%	1.70 years
60%	1.47 years
70%	1.31 years
80%	1.17 years
90%	1.08 years
100%	1.00 years

TRANSACTION: Deposit $10,000.00 at the specified interest rate, compounded annually. The equity will double to $20,000.00 in the associated time.

CHAPTER V

THE STANDARD BUILDING BLOCKS

5.1 BUILDING A PROFIT.

The profit characteristics of the four primary securities are presented in Chapter II. This discussion is centered around the description of the profit characteristics of the individual securities augmented by graphical representations.

The astute reader may have made two observations to this point. First, the horizontal axis of all graphs in Chapter II is the common stock price. Second, as a result of the discussions in Chapter IV, the vertical axis can be standardized to percent profit. Given both these observations, it follows that the basic securities can be combined mathematically to produce second order profit characteristics.

The thrust of this exercise is to produce a situation with inherently superior profit potential. Not all combined characteristics are superior. Those that are superior however exhibit a reduced risk of loss. The technique of combining profit characteristics is known in the market place as hedging.

Chapter III discussed the computation of the original value (OV) for the four basic securities of interest. The OV of component securities are combined to produce a total OV for the investment. This total OV is used in the profitability calculations described in Chapter IV. Similarly, the final value of the investment (FVI) used to determine percent profit (%P) is the total final value. It is necessary then to describe the FVI of component securities and their combination into the total FVI when hedging is employed.

The tools with which the reader has been provided thus far do not facilitate the analysis of the combination of securities in a hedge. If however the characteristics of the basic securities were described mathematically, simple techniques could be applied to determine the compound profit characteristics of any investment.

The goal of this chapter is to tie together the preceding four chapters and provide a standard method to measure profitability. The reader will be required to refer back to the preceding figures and tables as part of this process. While the references back to the preceding chapters may be annoying, the benefits in understanding will be well worth the effort. With this goal in mind, let us proceed to describe the standard building blocks in mathematical terms.

5.2 FINAL VALUE OF THE INVESTMENT.

There are two ways to describe the final value of the investment (FVI). The first and most straight forward is to simply multiply the assumed final price by the number of securities. This approach was applied in Chapter II to develop the final value curves of the four basic securities. The discussion in Chapter II evolved to a presentation of the profit characteristics of these component securities. Having determined profit (P) as a function of assumed stock price, the investor can determine FVI by adding original value (OV) and profit (P). This second method of computing FVI is superior to the first because it allows a more general handling of both long and short positions as well as the multiple security hedges.

In a hedge, FVI is the sum of the profit of each component security plus the original value of the total investment less commission and interest charges. The equation which describes this process is:

$$FVI = P_t + OV - C_t - M_i \qquad \text{(Eq 5-1)}$$

Where: FVI = Final Value of the Investment.

P_t = Total Profit on the Investment.

OV = Original Value of the Investment.

C_t = Total Commission (entry + exit) for the Transaction.

M_i = Margin Interest Charges.

The reader will note that the above calculation accounts for all commission and margin interest charges. Yield from dividends or convertible bond interest is also accounted in the total profit (P_t). As discussed in Chapter III, an end loading approximation has been selected to account for both yield and margin interest charges. While this approach is not completely accurate, the results vary only insignificantly from the most rigorous method.

The FVI equation can be applied to each investment situation. Using FVI in conjunction with the percent profit (%P) equation (Eq 4-1) the investor can standardize the profitability of a subject investment or hedge.

5.3 PROFIT FROM COMMON STOCK.

In the simplest case, an investment in common stock can be described through the parameters of the investment. It is necessary to preserve flexibility in this mathematical description so that it can be applied to hedges employing common stock as a component security. In addition, the equation must handle short as well as long positions. With these goals in mind, profit for an investment in common stock can be expressed as:

$$P_s = N * ((S - S_o) + Y_s) \qquad \text{(Eq 5-2)}$$

Where: P_s = Profit on an Investment in Stock.

N = Number of Shares Purchased.

S = Assumed Stock Price.

S_o = Initial Stock Price.

Y_s = Yield on a Share of Common Stock Prorated Over the Holding Period.

A negative value for the number of shares (N) is used to indicate a short position. A value of N equal to -100 shares would indicate a short sale of 100 shares of common stock.

> Consider the purchase of 150 shares of XYZ common stock for $14.00 per share with an entry commission of $39.22. The stock pays a dividend of $0.26 per share. The holding period for the investment is 40 weeks. The assumed stock price at liquidation is $20.00 resulting in the liquidation commission of $56.80. The transaction is accomplished on 100% margin.

In solving for the %P of the above investment the investor must first compute the value of P_s using equation 5-2.

$$P_s = 150 * ((\$20.00 - \$14.00) + \$0.20)$$

$$P_s = \$930.00$$

The next step in the process is to apply equation 3-2 to determine the OV.

$$OV_{100} = (150 * \$14.00 * 1.00) + \$39.22$$

$$OV_{100} = \$2139.22$$

Equation 5-1 is applied to determine FVI. Since the transaction is accomplished on 100% margin, there will be no margin interest charges (i.e. $M_i = 0$).

$$FVI = \$930.00 + \$2139.22 - \$96.02 - \$0.00$$

$$FVI = \$2973.20$$

As a result of the discussion in Chapter IV, the comparison between candidate investments is best made on the basis of effective annualized rate (%P). Applying equation 4-1 we have:

$$\%P = ((\$2973.20 \ / \ \$2139.22) - 1.0\ ) * 100 * (52/40)$$

$$\%P = 50.7\%$$

This process can be applied for several assumed stock prices. By plotting the results and drawing a line between the points a percent profit curve will be generated. The resultant graph will be similar in form to the graph displayed in Figure 2. Differences which exist are due to the variations between the parameters of the respective investments the fact that we now account for both commission and interest charges.

The reader is encouraged to solve for the value of %P for the assumed stock prices of $10.00 and $30.00 per share and plot these points along with the above results. By drawing a line between the points, the %P can be read from the graph for other values of assumed stock price. This technique of extrapolation will prove invaluable in reducing the computations associated with analysis of an investment.

5.4 PROFIT FROM CALL OPTIONS.

Calculating the profit characteristics for an investment in call options is a bit more sporting than the calculation for the common stock. As stated previously, the analysis of options centers on the option value at expiration. The computational difficulty is due to a discontinuity in the call option value curve which occurs at the exercise price. Figures 5 and 6 (pp 33, 34) portray this situation graphically. Due to the discontinuity in the option value curve, the final value (FV) of a call option must be expressed as a pair of equations. The selection of the equation which is applicable is based on the relative value of the assumed stock price and the option exercise price.

$$FV_c = \$0.00 \qquad \text{for } S < \text{or} = E \qquad \text{(Eq 5-3)}$$

or

$$FV_c = 100^*(S-E_c) \text{ for } S > E$$

Where: FV_c = Final Value of Call Option.

S = Assumed Stock Price at Expiration.

E_c = Exercise Price of the Call Option.

Once the FV_c has been determined, the profit on the call option can be computed in a similar manner to the equation used for the common stock.

$$P_o = N * (FV_o - O_p) \qquad \text{(Eq 5-4)}$$

Where: P_o = Profit on the Option.*

N = Number of Options.

FV_o = Final Value of the Option.

O_p = Option Price.

As was previously the case, a negative value of N is used to indicate a short position. In order to describe the short sale of 10 options, a value of N equal to -10 is entered in equation 5-4. The reader will note that equation 5-4 refers to options in general. The equation is in fact applicable to both put and call options.

---

*Note: P_o is expressed as P_c for call options and as P_p for put options.

> Consider the short sale of 1 call option on 100% margin for $200.00 with an exercise price of $15.00 and an underlying common stock selling for $12.00 per share. The option will expire in 26 weeks. The commission charge for the short sale is $25.00.

The exit commission for this investment is based on the value of the option at expiration. If the underlying common stock price is less than the exercise price at expiration, the option will expire worthless. An exit transaction will not be required and therefore the exit commission will be zero.

The ultimate goal of this exercise is to determine the percent profit for the investment. The process requires the investor to determine OV as described in Chapter III, P_0 and FVI as described above and finally %P by applying equation 4-1. The results of these computations are displayed in Table 8 for several; assumed stock prices. The reader is encouraged to plot the results of the analysis and thus generate the %P graph for this investment. The result will be similar to the curve displayed in Figure 6. (p. 34) Differences will exist due to the parameters of the respective investments.

5.5 PROFIT FROM PUT OPTIONS.

Calculating the profit characteristics of an investment in put options is similar to the process employed for call options. Like call options, the put also exhibits a discontinuity in the final value curve at the exercise price. Figures 8 and 9 (pp. 39, 40) portray this discontinuity. In order to describe the put option value curve at expiration, a pair of equations is required. The selection of the equation which is applicable is based on the relative position of the assumed stock price and the exercise price.

TABLE 8. %P FROM THE SALE OF A CALL OPTION.

OV = $75.00

STOCK PRICE CHANGE		−25%	0%	25%	50%	100%
ASSUMED STOCK PRICE	(S)	9.00	12.00	15.00	18.00	24.00
CALL FINAL VALUE	(FV_c)	0.00	0.00	0.00	300.00	900.00
PROFIT ON CALL OPT	(P_c)	200.00	200.00	200.00	−100.00	−700.00
MARGIN INTEREST	(M_i)	0.00	0.00	0.00	0.00	0.00
COMMISSION	(C_t)	−25.00	−25.00	−25.00	−50.00	−50.00
FINAL VALUE INVST	(FVI)	250.00	250.00	250.00	−75.00	−675.00
ANNUALIZED %P	(%P)	466.7%	466.7%	466.7%	−400.0%	−2000.0%

TRANSACTION: Sell 1 call option on 100% margin for $200.00 with an exercise price of $15.00 and an underlying common stock selling for $12.00 per share. The option will expire in 26 weeks. The commission charge for the short sale is $25.00.

$$FV_p = \$0.00 \qquad \text{for } S > E \qquad \text{(Eq 5-5)}$$

or

$$FV_p = 100^*(E_p - S) \quad \text{for } S < \text{or} = E$$

Where: FV_p = Final Value of the Put Option.

S = Assumed Stock Price.

E_p = Exercise Price of the Put Option.

Once FV_p has been determined, the profit on the put option (P_o) is computed using equation 5-4. The process to determine %P is the same as for call options. OV, P_o and FVI are computed as intermediate variables and applied to the %P equation 4-1.

> Consider the purchase of 2 put options for \$125.00 each with an exercise price of \$20.00. The underlying common stock price is \$20.00 per share at the time of the transaction. The entry commission is \$30.00. The option has 41 weeks to expiration.

The first step in the analysis of this investment is to compute the OV using equation 3-1.

$$OV_{100} = (2 * \$125.00 * 1.00) + \$30.00$$

$$OV_{100} = \$280.00$$

At this stage, the investor must select an assumed stock price. Since the discontinuity in the %P curve will occur at the exercise price, we will select \$20.00 for the assumed stock price. Equation 5-5 is then applied to determine the final value of the put.

$$FV_p = 100 * (\$20.00 - \$20.00)$$

$$FV_p = \$0.00$$

Applying equation 5-4, the profit on the put is determined.

$$P_o = 2 * (\$0.00 - \$125.00)$$

$$P_o = -\$250.00$$

Next, equation 5-1 is applied to determine the final value of the investment.

$$FVI = -\$250.00 + \$280.00 - \$30.00 - \$0.00$$

$$FVI = \$0.00$$

The reader will note that since the option expires worthless there is no exit commission in the above equation. Also, the equation may appear to be a convoluted way to determine that the option is worthless. This mechanization is necessary for the sake of generality. This same equation will apply for all possible outcomes of the investment. Finally, equation 4-1 is applied to determine the %P.

$$\%P = ((\ \$0.00 / \$280.00\ ) - 1.0\ ) * 100 * 52/41$$

$$\%P = -126.8\%$$

The above result may leave the reader with an uneasy feeling. Clearly, 126% of the investment has not been lost. Consider however that in this case the total investment was lost in 41 weeks. In accordance with our standard, the percent profit is annualized. Therefore losses as well as gains are amplified by the less than one year holding period of the example investment.

As before, the reader is encouraged to solve the example problem with other assumed stock prices. The results of this exercise are displayed in Table 9. The reader is encouraged to plot the results and compare the graph with Figure 8 on page 39.

TABLE 9. %P FROM THE PURCHASE OF PUT OPTIONS.

OV = $280.00

STOCK PRICE CHANGE		−50%	−25%	0%	25%	50%
ASSUMED STOCK PRICE	(S)	10.00	15.00	20.00	25.00	30.00
PUT FINAL VALUE	(FV_p)	1000.00	500.00	0.00	0.00	0.00
PROFIT ON PUT	(P_p)	1750.00	750.00	−250.00	−250.00	−250.00
MARGIN INTEREST	(M_i)	0.00	0.00	0.00	0.00	0.00
COMMISSION	(C_t)	−60.00	−60.00	−30.00	−30.00	−30.00
FINAL VALUE INVST	(FVI)	1970.00	970.00	0.00	0.00	0.00
ANNUALIZED %P	(%P)	765.5%	312.5%	−126.8%	−126.8%	−126.8%

TRANSACTION: Consider the purchase of 2 put options for $125.00 each with an exercise price of $20.00. The underlying common stock price is $20.00 per share at the time of the transaction. The entry commission is $30.00. The option has 41 weeks to expiration.

There is an important insight to be gained when dealing with naked option transactions. For the option buyer, there is a real risk of losing his full investment. For the option seller, the potential for loss is unlimited. The option investor must be prepared to exit from an option investment as it becomes unprofitable. Holding the position in the hope of a recovery may be catastrophic. A key factor to remember is that the option is an expiring asset and eventually the investor *must* run out of time.

5.6 PROFIT FROM CONVERTIBLE SECURITIES.

Dealing with convertible securities presents a new and interesting challenge. Since convertibles are not generally held to maturity, final value considerations are not normally relevant. We must think instead of the estimated convertible price as a function of the underlying stock price in much the same manner as presented in section 2.4. In this analysis, the convertible is generally several years from maturity thus its redemption value is not normally a factor. The convertible security's conversion value (CV) and investment value (IV) define the asymptotes to the price movement. The path which the convertible price follows however is hyperbolic and the CV and IV asymptotes are valid only in the extremes.

McKean (Ref 2), in conjunction with Samuelson (Ref 1), has provided a mathematical model which will describe the convertible security price as a function of underlying stock price. The model applies the parameters of the convertible security in conjunction with a gamma (G) variable to describe this relationship. The equation is stated below:

C = (((G-1)**(G-1)) / (G**G)) * IV *

((CR*S)/IV)**G) + IV (Eq 5-6)

$$C = \frac{(G - 1)^{(G - 1)}}{G^G} * IV * \left[\frac{CV * S}{IV}\right]^G + IV$$

Where: C = Convertible Security Price.

G = Gamma Constant for the Convertible Model.

IV = Investment Value.

CR = Conversion Ratio.

S = Assumed Stock Price.

The gamma model, which takes its name from the gamma variable in the equation, describes a family of curves which are bounded by the asymptotes CV and IV and by the equation:

$$C_+ = (CR * S) + IV \qquad \text{(Eq 5-7)}$$

Where: C_+ = Upper Limit Asymptote of Convertible Model.

CR = Conversion Ratio.

S = Assumed Stock Price.

IV = Investment Value.

The selection of the actual model curve and its associated gamma value from the family of possible solutions is based on the point defined by the current convertible security price and the associated current stock price. The gamma curve which passes through this point is the model for the particular convertible security under evaluation.

This situation is displayed graphically in Figure 12. The astute reader will recognize that equation 5-7, which defines the upper limit of the model, corresponds with the algebraic reduction of equation 5-6 with gamma set equal to one $(G = 1)$.

Gamma may assume any value which is greater than or equal to 1.0. In practice however, gamma rarely exceeds a magnitude of 4.0. As gamma increases in magnitude, the model curve approaches both the IV and CV asymptotes. The mechanism is thus provided to select a value of gamma which best models the subject convertible. Since the convertible is traded in the market place, the current value of all parameters in equation 5-6, with the exception of gamma, can be obtained from your broker. By inserting these values into the model the investor can solve for gamma using a trial and error approach. Having determined gamma, the model is established. The gamma value then becomes a constant in equation 5-6. By varying the stock price, the convertible price can be estimated by solving the model equation. Theoretically at least, the gamma value will be a constant for the subject convertible. There is one proviso. As you recall, investment value (IV) was used to determine gamma. If market conditions change, such as a rise in the prime rate, the convertible's IV will also change. This will effect the model and require the investor to recompute the value of gamma. Generally, a change in IV of more than 15% is required to significantly alter the results of the model.

There is no simple equation which expresses gamma as a function of S, IV, CR, and C. The determination of the value of gamma must be accomplished by an iterative process.

CONVERTIBLE VALUE VS. STOCK PRICE

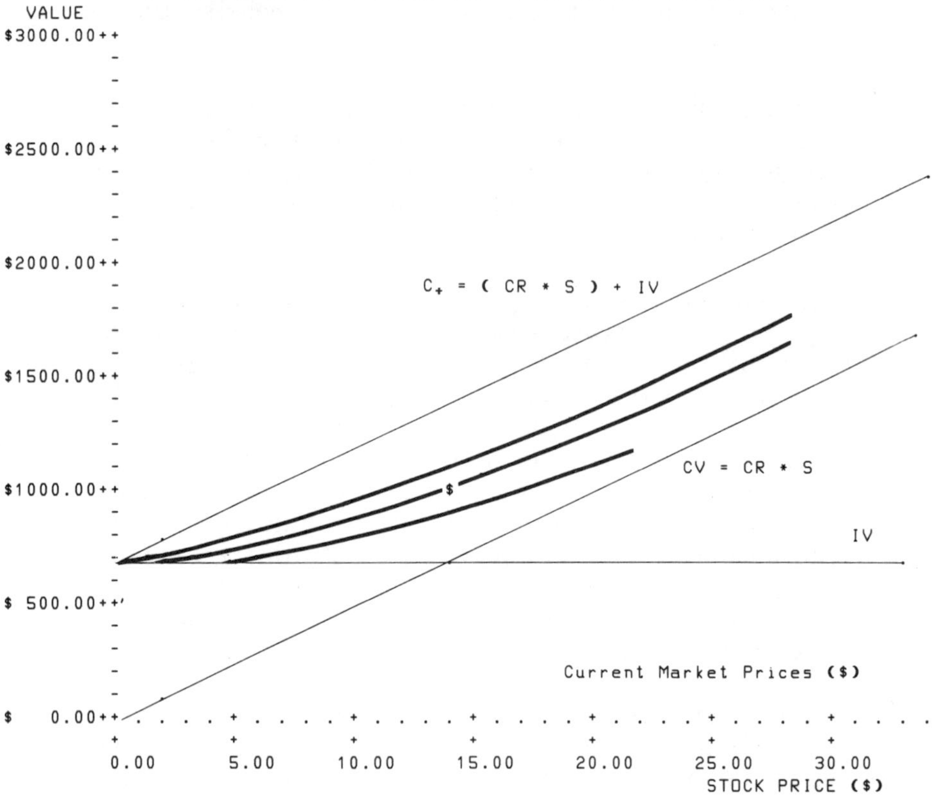

FIGURE 12. FAMILY OF GAMMA MODEL CURVES FOR A CONVERTIBLE SECURITY.

TRANSACTION: XYZ company convertible bond is convertible into 50 shares of common stock. The bond investment value is \$700.00. The current market value of the bond is \$1000.00 and the common stock price is \$14.00.

The process requires the investor to insert the current convertible security parameters into the model equation and guess at the value of gamma. The model equation is then solved for the convertible security price. The result is compared with the actual price. The process is repeated until the difference between the model result and the actual price is insignificant.

This trial and error process lends itself to the capabilities which are available in a programable calculator or a digital computer. The investor who does not have access to this capability should rely on the graphical technique discussed in Chapter II.

There is one further point which should be made. The gamma model is not truly hyperbolic in nature through its entire range. When applying the model, the investor must be careful to test the convergence of the model equation (Eq 5-6) with the conversion value (CV) asymptote. As the assumed stock price increases, the model will initially approach the CV asymptote. As the price increase continues, the model will begin to diverge from the asymptote. At this point and beyond, the convertible price should be modeled by using the conversion value directly.

The test required to verify convergence can be based on the relative magnitude of the gamma model's slope and to the slope of the conversion value (CV) asymptote. The conversion ratio (CR) is the slope of the conversion value asymptote. As long as the gamma model's slope is less than the conversion ratio, the gamma model is convergent. This test provides the necessary and sufficient condition for convergence of the gamma model.

An algebraic reduction of the test criteria can be achieved by taking advantage of the constraints on the variables involved. Specifically, all variables are positive and gamma is greater than or equal to 1.0. By applying the rules of algebra, the test criteria can be further reduced. The result is an equation which defines the assumed stock price at which the transition between the gamma model equation and the conversion value equation occurs.

$$TSP = (G / (G-1)) * (IV / CR) \qquad \text{(Eq 5-8)}$$

$$TSP = \frac{G}{(G - 1)} * \frac{IV}{CR}$$

Where: TSP = Transitional Assumed Stock Price.

G = Gamma Constant for the Convertible Model.

IV = Investment Value.

CR = Conversion Ratio.

The test for convergence is a simple matter of comparing the assumed stock price (S) with the transitional stock price (TSP) described by Equation 5-8. If S is less than TSP use the convertible security price as estimated by the gamma model equation (Eq 5-6). If S is greater than TSP, estimate the convertible security price to be equal to its conversion value (CV).

> Consider the purchase of 1 convertible bond for $1000.00 issued by XYZ company which is convertible into 50 shares of common stock. The bond pays an annual yield of $100.00 per year and has an investment value of $700.00. The current stock price is $14.00 per share. The entry and exit commission charge is $10.00 per bond. The holding period for the bond is 52 weeks.

Using the trial and error technique, Gamma is determined to be 1.408. Applying this factor as a constant in equation 5-6 and combining terms algebraically we have:

C = .4285 * 700.00*((50*S/700.00)**1.408)+700.00

or

C = 299.95 *((.07143 * S)**1.408) + 700.00

The above equation represents the convertible security price model as a function of the underlying stock price (S). Solving the equation for an assumed stock price of $7.00 per share results in an estimated convertible security value.

C = 299.95 *((.07143 * $7.00)**1.408) + 700.00

C = 299.95 *(0.3768) + 700.00

C = $813.03

The reader is encouraged to solve for other assumed values of stock price and to compare the results with those of Figure 11. (p. 45) Remember that if the assumed stock price is greater than the transitional stock price (TSP) the convertible security value is estimated to be its conversion value.

The direction of this analysis of convertible securities is ultimately aimed at the determination of %P. As was previously the case, the intermediate variables, P, OV, and FVI, must be determined.

The profit from an investment in convertible securities is computed using the estimated convertible security price. The equation which describes this relationship is similar in form to equation 5-2 which applies to common stock. The profit equation for convertible securities is:

$$P_{cv} = N * ((C - C_o) + Y_{cv}) \qquad \text{(Eq 5-9)}$$

Where: P_{cv} = Profit on an Investment in Convertible Securities.

N = Number of Convertibles.

C = Estimated Convertible Security Price.

C_o = Initial Convertible Security Price.

Y_{cv} = Annual Yield for the Convertible.

Applying equation 5-9 to the above example we have:

$$P_{cv} = 1 * ((\$813.00 - \$1000.00) + \$100.00)$$

$$P_{cv} = -\$87.00$$

In order to determine the final value, the original value (OV) must be computed. Applying equation 3-1 we have:

$$OV_{100} = (1 * \$1000.00 * 1.00) + \$10.00$$

$$OV_{100} = \$1010.00$$

Next, applying equation 5-1 yields the final value of the investment.

$$FVI = -\$87.00 + \$1010.00 - \$20.00 - \$0.00$$

$$FVI = \$903.00$$

Finally, %P is determined using equation 4-1.

$$\%P = ((\$903.00/\$1010.00)-1.0) * 100 * 52/52$$

$$\%P = -10.6\%$$

This process can be extended through other assumed stock prices and developed into a percent profit (%P) curve. The results of this extension are contained in Table 10. The reader will note that the convertible security is described in terms of its percent profit as a function of the underlying stock price. The gamma model is required to estimate the convertible security price which is applied to the profit equation. The estimated convertible security price represents an intermediate variable in the %P calculation. While the gamma model is the more elegant approach to tying the convertible security price to the stock price, the graphical technique described in Chapter II is also acceptable.

TABLE 10. %P FROM THE PURCHASE OF CONVERTIBLE SECURITY.

$OV_{100} = \$1010.00$ $G = 1.408$

STOCK PRICE CHANGE		−50%	−25%	0%	25%	50%
ASSUMED STOCK PRICE	(S)	7.00	10.50	14.00	17.50	21.00
EST. CONV PRICE	(C)	813.00	900.06	1000.70	1109.85	1230.86
YIELD FROM CONV.	(Y_{cv})	100.00	100.00	100.00	100.00	100.00
PROFIT ON CONV.	(P_{cv})	−87.00	0.06	100.70	209.85	330.86
MARGIN INTEREST	(M_i)	0.00	0.00	0.00	0.00	0.00
COMMISSION	(C_t)	−20.00	−20.00	−20.00	−20.00	−20.00
FINAL VALUE INVST	(FVI)	903.00	990.06	1090.71	1199.85	1320.86
ANNUALIZED %P	(%P)	−10.6%	−2.0%	8.0%	18.8%	30.8%

TRANSACTION: Consider the purchase of 1 convertible bond for $1000.00 issued by XYZ company which is convertible into 50 shares of common stock. The bond pays an annual yield of $100.00 per year and has an investment value of $700.00. The current stock price is $14.00 per share. The entry and exit commission charge is $10.00 per bond. The holding period of the convertible is 52 weeks.

CHAPTER VI

THE SUM IS SUPERIOR

6.1 IT ALL ADDS UP.

To this point, we have examined the component securities and analyzed their profit characteristics. The most important quality of this discussion is it's mathematical irrefutability. Given the nature of the component securities and an assumed stock price, the profitability of the investment is deterministic.

We have gone to great lengths to establish annualized percent profit (%P) as a consistent standard of measure of profitability and also to define profit as a function of a single variable, the common stock price. By so doing, it is possible to combine investments in component securities to produce a compound profit situation or a hedge. Since this combination is performed within prescribed mathematical limits, the resultant profit characteristic is also deterministic and irrefutable.

A key issue, for the reader, is to understand the equivalence of both simple investments and hedges in terms of their profit characteristics. The investor may well be comfortable with profit curves of component securities. At the same time however, the combined characteristics of a hedge may seem alien. There is no more magic to hedging than there is to the statement that "two plus three equals five."

The profit curves of component securities are predetermined by their inherent terms and conditions. Likewise, the profit characteristics of a hedge are also predetermined by the proportional combination of the terms and conditions of the component securities to construct the hedge profit characteristics. The balance of this chapter will present several of the more common hedge types. These are by no means an exhaustive set of possibilities but rather a presentation of likely situations.

6.2 STOCK / CALL HEDGE.

The stock/call hedge, as its name implies, involves the purchase of common stock and the simultaneous sale of call options. The time period of the hedge is constrained by the expiration date of the option. The combination of long the stock and short the call option results in a profit curve which is triangular in form. The triangle can be skewed by modifying the ratio of shares purchased to calls sold. As relatively more shares are purchased, the hedge will be skewed to be more profitable on the up side of the common stock price. Likewise, as relatively less shares are purchased, the reverse is true and the hedge will be skewed to be more profitable on the down side of common stock price.

> Consider the purchase of 500 shares of XYZ company at $23.00 per share and the sale of 10 call options for $300.00 with an exercise price of $25.00 and an expiration date which is 35 weeks hence. The stock pays a dividend of $0.50 per share. The entry commission is $340.00 and the current margin interest rate is 13.50%.

Table 11 contains the combination of the component securities into the hedge. Figure 13 displays the resultant profit curve. There is no magic to the generation of the profit curve. The profit for the investment is simply the sum of the profit from each of the component securities, given an assumed stock price. This process is tabulated, for five assumed stock price values, in the columns of Table 11. The graph displayed in Figure 13 is simply a pictorial representation of the assumed stock price (top line of Table 11) vs. the percent profit (bottom line of Table 11).

The reader will note that a constant value for both commission and margin is applied across all assumed stock prices. Use of a constant value simplifies the calculations while creating an acceptably small error in the results. A constant margin interest charge implies that the debit balance (DB) will remain unchanged over the duration of the hedge. Since the DB moves up and down with fluctuations in the market some offsetting effects can be anticipated. On the basis of experience, a constant DB is a reasonable assumption. The exit commission estimate implies that the option will expire worthless. Therefore, an exit transaction for the option will not be required. In practice, this situation occurs often. This feature, coupled with creative techniques to exit the hedge makes this commission simplification acceptable. A discussion of these creative techniques will be presented in Chapter X.

TABLE 11. STOCK / CALL HEDGE.

OV_{50} = \$5540.00 DB = \$3300.00

STOCK PRICE CHANGE		−50%	−25%	0%	25%	50%
ASSUMED STOCK PRICE	(S)	11.50	17.20	23.00	28.70	34.50
CALL A FINAL VALUE	(FV_{ca})	0.00	0.00	0.00	370.00	950.00
YIELD FROM STOCK	(Y_s)	0.336	0.336	0.336	0.336	0.336
PROFIT ON THE STOCK	(P_s)	−5581.73	−2731.73	168.27	3018.27	5918.27
PROFIT ON CALL A	(P_{ca})	3000.00	3000.00	3000.00	−700.00	−6500.00
MARGIN INTEREST	(M_i)	−300.00	−300.00	−300.00	−300.00	−300.00
COMMISSION	(C_t)	−555.00	−555.00	−555.00	−555.00	−555.00
FINAL VALUE INVST	(FVI)	2103.27	4953.27	7853.27	7003.27	4103.27
ANNUALIZED %P	(%P)	−92.2%	−15.7%	62.0%	39.2%	−38.5%

TRANSACTION: Buy 500 shares of XYZ company at \$23.00 per share and sell 10 call options for \$300.00 each with an exercise price of \$25.00 and an expiration date which is 35 weeks hence. The stock pays an annual dividend of \$0.50 per share. The entry commission is \$340.00 and the current margin interest rate is 13.50%.

PERCENT PROFIT VS. STOCK PRICE.

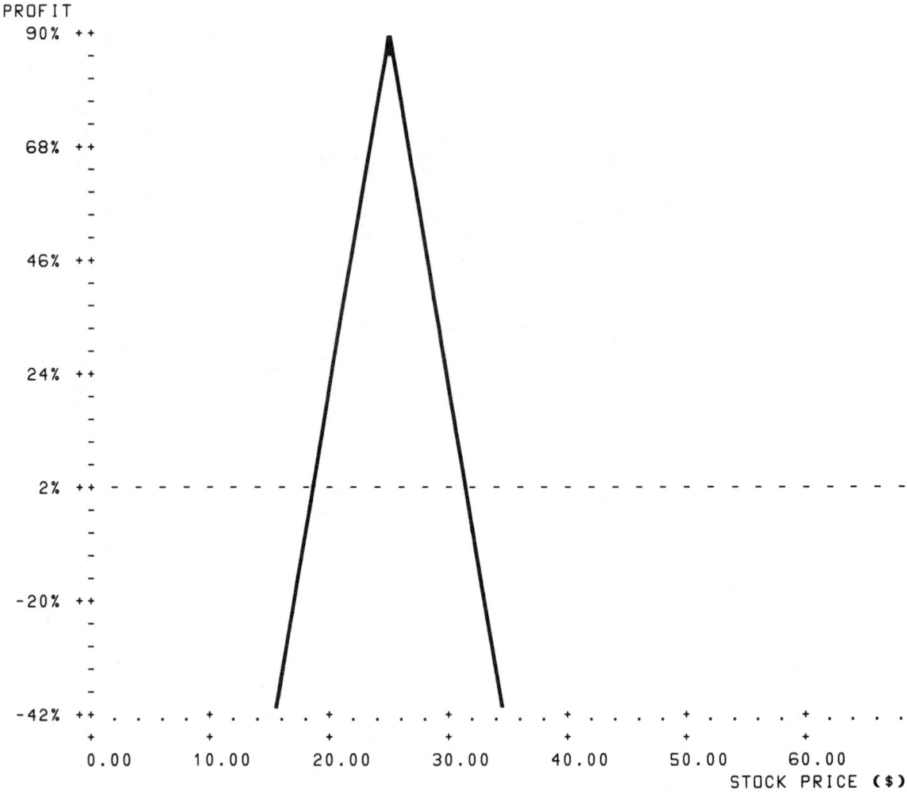

FIGURE 13. STOCK / CALL HEDGE.

TRANSACTION: Buy 500 shares of XYZ company at $23.00 per share and sell 10 call options for $300.00 each with an exercise price of $25.00 and an expiration date which is 35 weeks hence. The stock pays an annual dividend of $0.50 per share. The entry commission is $340.00 and the current margin interest rate is 13.50%.

6.3 CALL / STOCK / CALL HEDGE.

The call/stock/call hedge is an extension of the previously discussed stock/call hedge. This hedge is constructed by selecting two call options which differ in exercise price but have the same expiration date. The investor simultaneously purchases a number of shares of stock and sells call options for nominally twice the long position. Usually, the quantity of calls sold are split evenly between the two candidate options.

The resultant profit curve from this hedge is trapezoidal. Modifying the proportional relationship of the component securities will distort the basic shape of the curve.

> Consider the purchase of 500 shares of XYZ common stock for $23.00 per share, sell 5 call options for $300.00 each with an exercise price of $30.00, and sell 5 call options for $500.00 each with an exercise price of $20.00. Both options have 35 weeks remaining until expiration. The stock pays an annual dividend of $0.50. The entry commission is $370.00.

Table 12 and Figure 14 contain the results of the analysis of the above example. The profit curve for Figure 14 differs from the stock/call hedge in that the maximum profit is significantly lower. However, while the maximum profit is lower, the call/stock/call hedge maintains its maximum value over a broad range of common stock prices.

TABLE 12. CALL / STOCK / CALL HEDGE.

OV_{100} = $7870.00

STOCK PRICE CHANGE		−50%	−25%	0%	25%	50%
ASSUMED STOCK PRICE	(S)	11.50	17.20	23.00	28.70	34.50
CALL A FINAL VALUE	(FV_{ca})	0.00	0.00	300.00	870.00	1450.00
CALL B FINAL VALUE	(FV_{cb})	0.00	0.00	0.00	0.00	450.00
YIELD FROM STOCK	(Y_s)	0.336	0.336	0.336	0.336	0.336
PROFIT ON THE STOCK	(P_s)	−5581.73	−2731.73	168.27	3018.27	5918.27
PROFIT ON CALL A	(P_{ca})	2500.00	2500.00	1000.00	−1850.00	−4750.00
PROFIT ON CALL B	(P_{cb})	1500.00	1500.00	1500.00	1500.00	−750.00
MARGIN INTEREST	(M_i)	0.00	0.00	0.00	0.00	0.00
COMMISSION	(C_t)	−740.00	−740.00	−740.00	−740.00	−740.00
FINAL VALUE INVST	(FVI)	5548.27	8398.27	9798.27	9798.27	7548.27
ANNUALIZED %P	(%P)	−43.8%	10.0%	36.4%	36.4%	−6.1%

TRANSACTION:Buy 500 shares of XYZ common stock for $23.00 per share, sell 5 call options for $300.00 each with an exercise price of $30.00, and sell 5 call options for $500.00 each with an exercise price of $20.00. Both options have 35 weeks remaining until expiration. The stock pays an annual dividend of $0.50. The entry commission is $370.00.

PERCENT PROFIT VS. STOCK PRICE.

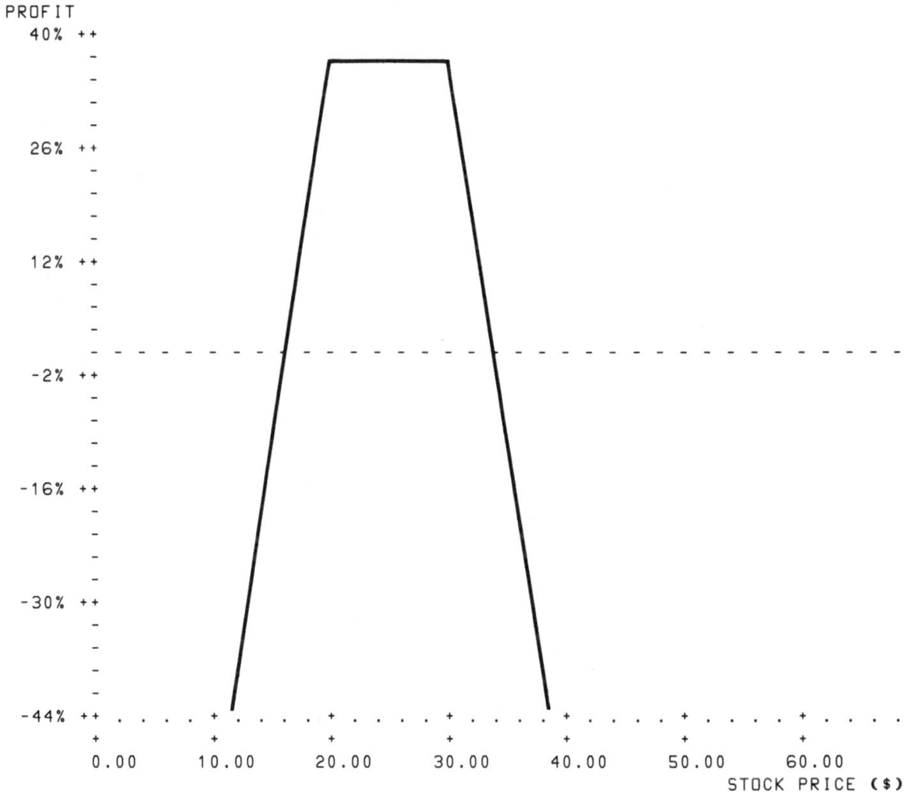

FIGURE 14. CALL / STOCK / CALL HEDGE.

TRANSACTION: Buy 500 shares of XYZ common stock for $23.00 per share, sell 5 call options for $300.00 each with an exercise price of $30.00, and sell 5 call options for $500.00 each with an exercise price of $20.00. Both options have 35 weeks remaining until expiration. The stock pays an annual dividend of $0.50. The entry commission is $370.00.

6.4 PUT / STOCK HEDGE.

The put/stock hedge is established by simultaneously purchasing put options and common stock. The characteristics of both securities are remarkably complementary. The put option buyer realizes his profit when the stock price falls and on the up side, he can only incur a fixed loss. The common stock is linear in nature and profits or losses are proportional to the movement in the common stock price. The purchase of put options in conjunction with common stock can be compared with the purchase of investment term insurance against a down side move in the common stock price. The profit curve of the put/stock hedge forms a "V" shape.

> Consider the purchase of 500 shares of XYZ common stock at $23.00 per share and the purchase of 10 put options for $300.00 each with an exercise price of $25.00. The stock pays a dividend of $0.50 per share and the option has 35 weeks until expiration. The entry commission is $340.00. The margin interest rate is 13.5%.

Table 13 and Figure 15 display the results of the analysis of the above example. Changes in the ratio of put options and common stock predominately affect the left side of the curve. At issue is how much insurance will be purchased. There is of course the possibility that the investment can be "over-insured" to provide a profit in the event of a downward move in the common stock price. The above example presents the "over-insured" case.

TABLE 13. PUT / STOCK HEDGE.

OV_{50} = $9090.00 DB = $5750.00

STOCK PRICE CHANGE		−50%	−25%	0%	25%	50%
ASSUMED STOCK PRICE	(S)	11.50	17.20	23.00	28.70	34.50
PUT FINAL VALUE	(FV_p)	1350.00	780.00	200.00	0.00	0.00
YIELD FROM STOCK	(Y_s)	0.336	0.336	0.336	0.336	0.336
PROFIT ON THE STOCK	(P_s)	−5581.73	−2731.73	168.27	3018.27	5918.27
PROFIT ON PUT	(P_p)	10500.00	4800.00	−1000.00	−3000.00	−3000.00
MARGIN INTEREST	(M_i)	−530.00	−530.00	−530.00	−530.00	−530.00
COMMISSION	(C_t)	−680.00	−680.00	−680.00	−680.00	−680.00
FINAL VALUE INVST	(FVI)	12798.27	9948.27	7048.27	7898.27	10798.27
ANNUALIZED %P	(%P)	60.6%	14.0%	−33.4%	−19.5%	27.9%

TRANSACTION: Buy 500 shares of XYZ common stock at $23.00 per share and buy 10 put options for $300.00 each with an exercise price of $25.00. The stock pays a dividend of $0.50 per share and the option has 35 weeks until expiration. The entry commission is $340.00. The margin interest rate is 13.5%.

PERCENT PROFIT VS. STOCK PRICE.

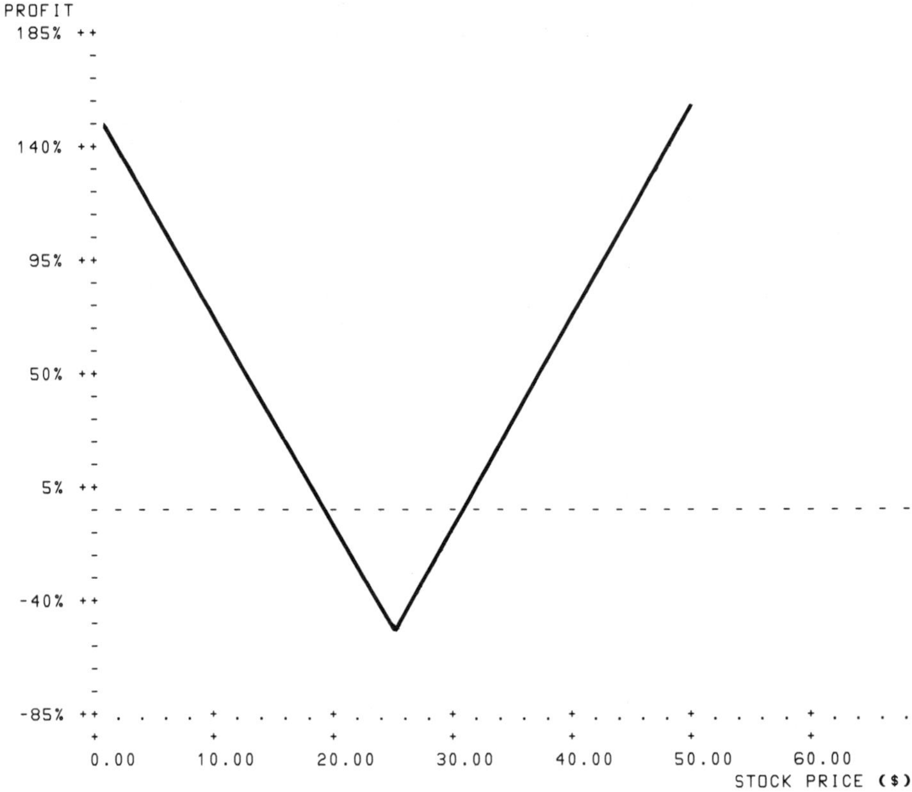

FIGURE 15. PUT / STOCK HEDGE.

TRANSACTION: Buy 500 shares of XYZ common stock at $23.00 per share and buy 10 put options for $300.00 each with an exercise price of $25.00. The stock pays a dividend of $0.50 per share and the option has 35 weeks until expiration. The entry commission is $340.00. The margin interest rate is 13.5%.

6.5 CONVERTIBLE / CALL HEDGE.

The convertible/call option hedge involves the simultaneous purchase of convertible securities and the sale of call options. Like the stock/call hedge, the profit curve is generally triangular in shape. The left side of the triangle curves upward in conformance with the profit characteristics of the convertible security.

> Consider the purchase of 20 XYZ company convertible bonds at $950.00 each. The bond has an investment value of $800.00 and a conversion ratio of 40 shares. The bond pays an annual yield of $120.00. Sell 12 call options for $400.00 each with an exercise price of $20.00. The current common stock price is $20.00 per share. The option has 35 weeks of life remaining. The current margin interest rate is 13.5%. The entry commission is $330.00.

Table 14 and Figure 16 display both the analysis and the resultant profit curve of the hedge. The convertible security price was estimated using the gamma model presented in Chapter V. Changes in the ratio of call options and convertible securities will skew the profit curve toward the profitable portion of the dominant component security. This operates in much the same manner as described for the stock/call hedge.

TABLE 14. CALL / CONVERTIBLE HEDGE.

OV[50] = $7430.00 G = 2.488 DB = $7100.00

STOCK PRICE CHANGE		−50%	−25%	0%	25%	50%
ASSUMED STOCK PRICE	(S)	10.00	15.00	20.00	25.00	30.00
EST. CONV PRICE	(C)	826.52	873.17	950.14	1060.09	1210.38
CALL A FINAL VALUE	(FV_{ca})	0.00	0.00	0.00	500.00	1000.00
YIELD FROM CONV.	(Y_{cv})	80.77	80.77	80.77	80.77	80.77
PROFIT ON CONV.	(P_{cv})	−854.20	78.80	1618.11	3817.25	6822.89
PROFIT ON CALL A	(P_{ca})	4800.00	4800.00	4800.00	−1200.00	−7200.00
MARGIN INTEREST	(M_i)	−645.00	−645.00	−645.00	−645.00	−645.00
COMMISSION	(C_t)	−505.00	−505.00	−505.00	−505.00	−505.00
FINAL VALUE INVST	(FVI)	10225.80	11158.81	12668.11	8909.25	5902.89
ANNUALIZED %P	(%P)	55.9%	74.6%	104.7%	29.9%	−30.5%

TRANSACTION: Buy 20 XYZ company convertible bonds at $950.00 each. The bond has an investment value of $800.00 and a conversion ratio of 40 shares. The bond pays an annual yield of $120.00. Sell 12 call options for $400.00 each with an exercise price of $15.00. The current common stock price is $20.00 per share. The option has 35 weeks of life remaining. The current margin interest rate is 13.5%. The entry commission is $330.00.

PERCENT PROFIT VS. STOCK PRICE.

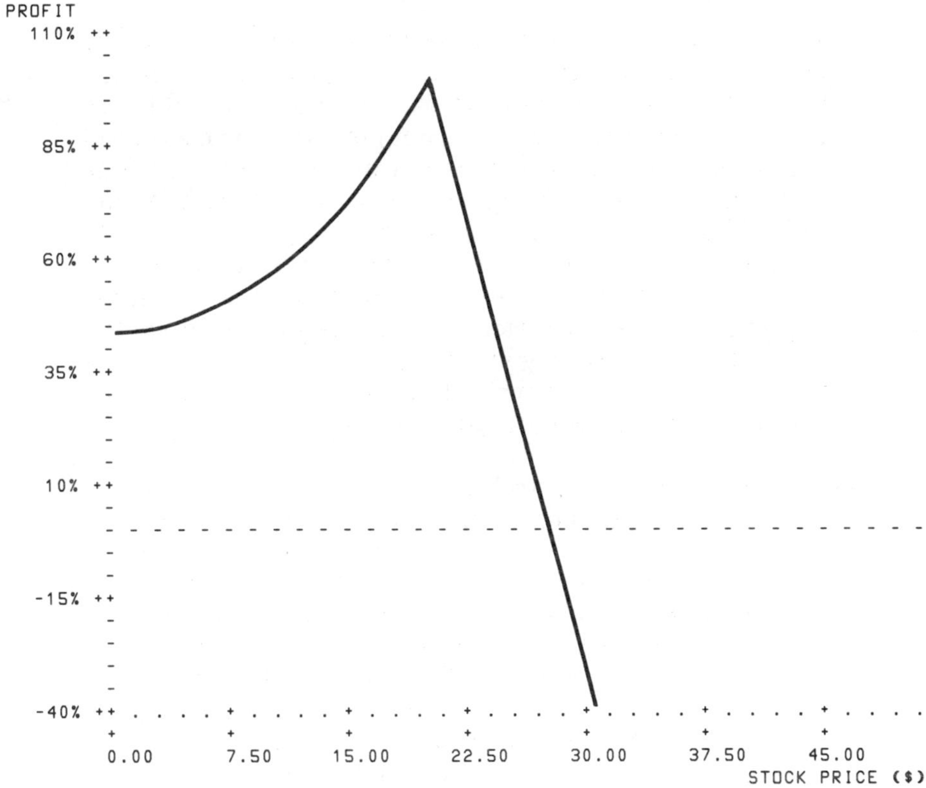

FIGURE 16. CALL / CONVERTIBLE HEDGE.

TRANSACTION: Buy 20 XYZ company convertible bonds at $950.00 each. The bond has an investment value of $800.00 and a conversion ratio of 40 shares. The bond pays an annual yield of $120.00. Sell 12 call options for $400.00 each with an exercise price of $20.00. The current common stock price is $20.00 per share. The option has 35 weeks of life remaining. The current margin interest rate is 13.5%. The entry commission is $330.00.

6.6 CALL / CONVERTIBLE / CALL HEDGE.

The nature of convertible securities provides greater flexibility in the ratio of long to short position in a hedge. Since the down side characteristics of a convertible are less vulnerable to loss than common stock, the shape of the composite investment is not piece-wise linear. The call/convertible/call hedge demonstrates this phenomenon. Like the call/stock/call hedge, options are sold against the equivalent long position in the security. As was previously the case, both options have the same expiration date but different exercise prices. Since the convertible inherently exhibits superior down side protection the ratio of total short call options need not be the 2:1 employed in the call/stock/call hedge.

> Consider the purchase of 20 XYZ company convertible bonds for $950.00 each. The bonds have an investment value of $800.00 and are convertible into 40 shares of common stock. The bond's yield is $120.00 per year. Sell 6 call options at $150.00 each with an exercise price of $25.00. Sell 6 call options for $400.00 each with an exercise price of $20.00. The current stock price is $20.00 per share. Both the options have 35 weeks of life remaining. The margin interest rate is 13.5%. The entry commission is $335.00.

The analysis of the profit characteristics of the above hedge is provided in Table 15. The corresponding profit characteristics is displayed in Figure 17. The reader will observe that the figure is vaguely trapezoidal. The curvature on the left side is due to the convertible's down side characteristics. The skew of the curve is due primarily to the ratio adjustment from the nominal 2:1 (total short to equivalent long).

TABLE 15. CALL / CONVERTIBLE / CALL HEDGE.

OV[50] = $7535.00 G = 2.488 DB = $8500.00

STOCK PRICE CHANGE		–50%	–25%	0%	25%	50%
ASSUMED STOCK PRICE	(S)	10.00	15.00	20.00	25.00	30.00
EST. CONV PRICE	(C)	826.52	873.17	950.14	1060.09	1210.87
CALL A FINAL VALUE	(FV_{ca})	0.00	0.00	0.00	500.00	1000.00
CALL B FINAL VALUE	(FV_{cb})	0.00	0.00	0.00	0.00	500.00
YIELD FROM CONV.	(Y_{cv})	80.77	80.77	80.77	80.77	80.77
PROFIT ON CONV.	(P_{cv})	–854.19	78.80	1618.11	3817.25	6822.89
PROFIT ON CALL A	(P_{ca})	2400.00	2400.00	2400.00	–600.00	–3600.00
PROFIT ON CALL B	(P_{cb})	900.00	900.00	900.00	900.00	–2100.00
MARGIN INTEREST	(M_i)	–770.00	–770.00	–770.00	–770.00	–770.00
COMMISSION	(C_t)	–585.00	–585.00	–585.00	–585.00	–585.00
FINAL VALUE INVST	(FVI)	8625.80	9558.80	11098.11	10297.25	7302.89
ANNUALIZED %P	(%P)	21.5%	39.9%	70.0%	54.8%	–4.6%

TRANSACTION: Buy 20 XYZ company convertible bonds for $950.00 each. The bonds have an investment value of $800.00 and are convertible into 40 shares of common stock. The bond's yield is $120.00 per year. Sell 6 call options at $150.00 each with an exercise price of $25.00. Sell 6 call options for $400.00 each with an exercise price of $20.00. The current stock price is $20.00 per share. Both the options have 35 weeks of life remaining. The margin interest rate is 13.5%. The entry commission is $335.00.

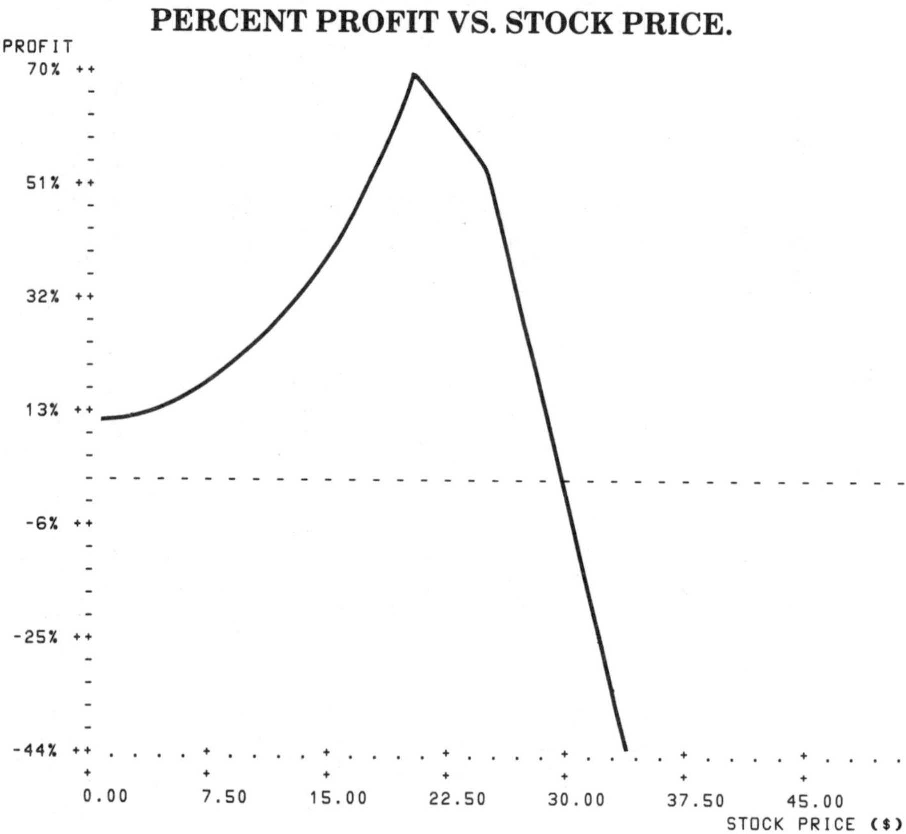

FIGURE 17. CALL / CONVERTIBLE / CALL HEDGE

TRANSACTION: Buy 20 XYZ company convertible bonds for $950.00 each. The bonds have an investment value of $800.00 and are convertible into 40 shares of common stock. The bond's yield is $120.00 per year. Sell 6 call options at $150.00 each with an exercise price of $25.00. Sell 6 call options for $400.00 each with an exercise price of $20.00. The current stock price is $20.00 per share. Both the options have 35 weeks of life remaining. The margin interest rate is 13.5%. The entry commission is $335.00.

6.7 PUT / CONVERTIBLE HEDGE.

The put/convertible hedge is a close cousin to the put/stock hedge. The main difference in the profit characteristics is due to the superior down side performance of a convertible security. As before, the purchase of put options can be compared to the purchase of term insurance against a down side move in the common stock price. The convertible security's inherent limit on down side loss reduces the number of put options required to protect the convertible.

> Consider the purchase of 20 XYZ company convertible bonds for $950.00 each. The bonds have an investment value of $800.00 and are convertible into 40 shares of common stock. The bond's yield is $120.00 per year. Buy 4 put options for $250.00 each with an exercise price of $15.00. The current common stock price is $20.00 per share. The option has 35 weeks until expiration. The entry commission is $228.00.

The analysis of the above example is contained in Table 16 and the profit curve is displayed in Figure 18. Adjustment of the ratio of put options to equivalent shares will cause a shift in the curve with respect to the zero line. As more puts are purchased, a larger up-side move in the common stock price is required for the hedge to be profitable. At the same time however, a larger holding of put options makes a down side move in the common stock more profitable.

TABLE 16. PUT / CONVERTIBLE HEDGE.

OV_{100} = \$20228.00 G = 2.428

STOCK PRICE CHANGE		−50%	−25%	0%	25%	50%
ASSUMED STOCK PRICE	(S)	10.00	15.00	20.00	25.00	30.00
EST. CONV PRICE	(C)	826.52	873.17	950.14	1060.09	1210.38
PUT FINAL VALUE	(FV_p)	500.00	0.00	0.00	0.00	0.00
YIELD FROM CONV.	(Y_{cv})	80.77	80.77	80.77	80.77	80.77
PROFIT ON CONV.	(P_{cv})	−854.20	78.80	1618.11	3817.25	6822.89
PROFIT ON PUT	(P_p)	1000.00	−1000.00	−1000.00	−1000.00	−1000.00
MARGIN INTEREST	(M_i)	0.00	0.00	0.00	0.00	0.00
COMMISSION	(C_t)	−403.00	−403.00	−403.00	−403.00	−403.00
FINAL VALUE INVST	(FVI)	19970.80	18903.80	20443.12	22642.25	25647.89
ANNUALIZED %P	(%P)	−1.9%	−9.7%	1.6%	17.7%	39.8%

TRANSACTION: Buy 20 XYZ company convertible bonds for \$950.00 each. The bonds have an investment value of \$800.00 and are convertible into 40 shares of common stock. The bond's yield is \$120.00 per year. Buy 4 put options for \$250.00 each with an exercise price of \$15.00. The current common stock price is \$20.00 per share. The option has 35 weeks until expiration. The entry commission is \$228.00.

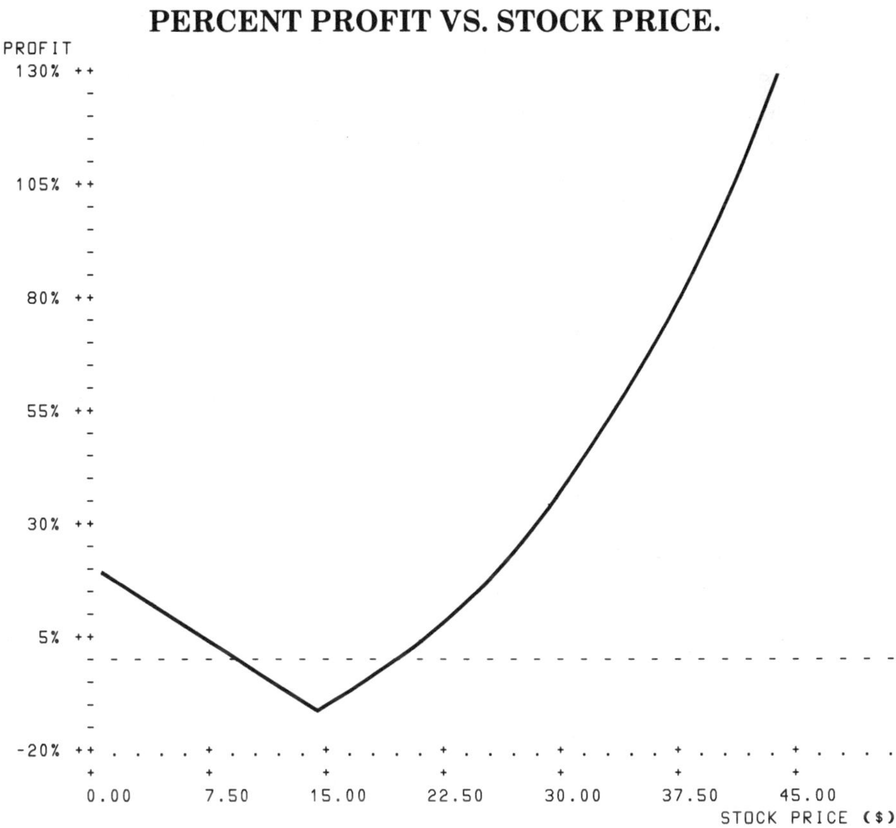

FIGURE 18. PUT / CONVERTIBLE HEDGE.

TRANSACTION: Buy 20 XYZ company convertible bonds for $950.00 each. The bonds have an investment value of $800.00 and are convertible into 40 shares of common stock. The bond's yield is $120.00 per year. Buy 4 put options for $250.00 each with an exercise price of $15.00. The current common stock price is $20.00 per share. The option has 35 weeks until expiration. The entry commission is $228.00.

6.8 CONVERTIBLE / STOCK HEDGE.

The convertible/stock hedge is one of the first forms of hedging. The hedge is created by selling common stock against a long position in convertible securities. Nominally, a 1:2 ratio of short to equivalent long position is established. The short position compensates for the down side vulnerability of the convertible at the expense of up side potential.

> Consider the purchase of 20 XYZ company convertible bonds for $950.00 each. The bond has an investment value of $800.00 and a conversion ratio of 40 shares of common stock. The bond's yield is $120.00 per year. Sell 200 shares of XYZ company common stock at $19.00 per share. The stock pays a dividend of $0.50 per share. The holding period for the hedge is arbitrarily set to one year. The margin interest rate is 13.5% and the entry commission is $270.00.

The results of the analysis of the above example is contained in Table 17. A graphical representation of these results is displayed in Figure 19. The stock/convertible hedge is common in many respects to the put/convertible hedge. While both provide down side protection, the stock/convertible has no expiration constraint. This longevity feature is achieved at the expense of up side potential of the hedge.

Since there is no fixed expiration period, a time period must be arbitrarily assumed in order to perform the calculation of %P. A one year period is a reasonable choice in the light of experience.

TABLE 17. CONVERTIBLE / STOCK HEDGE.

OV_{50} = \$9770.00 G = 2.269 DB = \$9500.00

STOCK PRICE CHANGE		−50%	−25%	0%	25%	50%
ASSUMED STOCK PRICE	(S)	9.50	14.25	19.00	23.75	28.50
EST. CONV PRICE	(C)	831.34	887.17	949.69	1049.69	1176.72
YIELD FROM STOCK	(Y_s)	0.50	0.50	0.50	0.50	0.50
YIELD FROM CONV.	(Y_{cv})	120.00	120.00	120.00	120.00	120.00
PROFIT ON THE STOCK	(P_s)	1800.00	850.00	−100.00	−1050.00	−2000.00
PROFIT ON CONV.	(P_{cv})	26.76	963.34	2393.80	4393.80	6934.34
MARGIN INTEREST	(M_i)	−1280.00	−1280.00	−1280.00	−1280.00	−1280.00
COMMISSION	(C_t)	−540.00	−540.00	−540.00	−540.00	−540.00
FINAL VALUE INVST	(FVI)	9776.78	9763.34	10243.80	11283.80	12884.34
ANNUALIZED %P	(%P)	0.1%	−0.1%	4.8%	15.5%	31.9%

TRANSACTION: Buy 20 XYZ company convertible bonds for \$950.00 each. The bond has an investment value of \$800.00 and a conversion ratio of 40 shares of common stock. The bond's yield is \$120.00 per year. Sell 200 shares of XYZ company common stock at \$19.00 per share. The stock pays a dividend of \$0.50 per share. The holding period for the hedge is arbitrarily set to one year. The margin interest rate is 13.5% and the entry commission is \$270.00.

PERCENT PROFIT VS. STOCK PRICE.

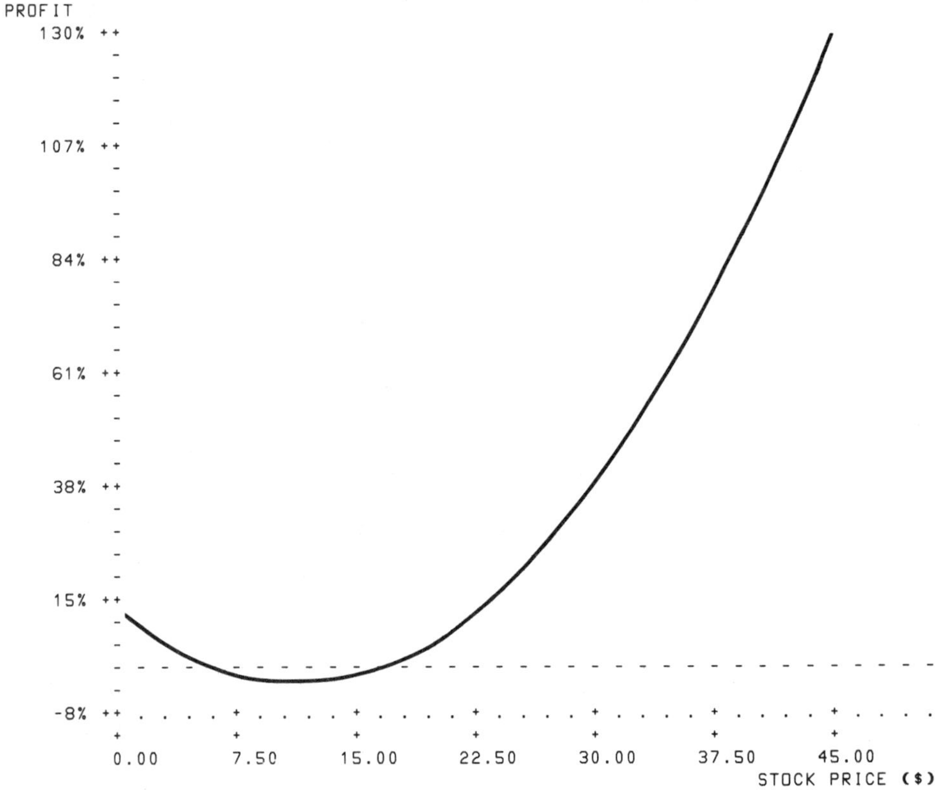

FIGURE 19. CONVERTIBLE / STOCK HEDGE.

TRANSACTION: Buy 20 XYZ company convertible bonds for $950.00 each. The bond has an investment value of $800.00 and a conversion ratio of 40 shares of common stock. The bond's yield is $120.00 per year. Sell 200 shares of XYZ company common stock at $19.00 per share. The stock pays a dividend of $0.50 per share. The holding period for the hedge is arbitrarily set to one year. The margin interest rate is 13.5% and the entry commission is $270.00.

6.9 OTHER HEDGES.

The reader is invited to let his imagination run wild. To this point, we have evaluated some of the basic combinations of component securities. The first level of departure from the discussion is to try different combinations of the component securities, such as the put/convertible/call hedge. Further, options with different expiration dates could be combined to produce more intriguing profit characteristics. Charell (Ref 5) discusses many of the possible variations in his book. The reader is encouraged to pursue alternate hedges. The major thrust of this effort however, should be directed to the generation of the hedge profit characteristics. By reducing all the candidate investments to the common measure of %P vs. stock price, the basis of comparison is established.

There yet remains one pressing question. That question is tied immutably to risk. We have defined the profit characteristics; but, at what risk?

CHAPTER VII

THE QUESTION

7.1 RISK.

Once the profit characteristics of an investment are known, risk assessment is the next and most important consideration. In simple terms, a potential profit must be weighted against the chance of achieving that profit. A fair bet is one which pays proportionally to the risk of the wager. As a minimum, we will accept nothing less than a fair bet. Ideally, we would like an investment which is weighted in our favor.

Many states run a form of the numbers game. In the simplest case, the participant or investor selects a three digit number. On the day of the competition, the state uses a random technique to generate the winning three digit number. Mathematically, the odds of the participant guessing the number *a priori* are one in a thousand. A fair pay off for the wager therefore is one thousand to one. Since most states pay much less than this, continued participation in the game must result in a net flow of capital from the participants to the state. In short, playing the numbers game is not a good investment.

A conscientious investor seeks investment situations which consistently place the odds in his favor. For comparison, let us select a base line investment in some form of federally guaranteed savings account. In this case, the return of the investors principal is guaranteed and he is essentially assured of the interest on his investment. The two primary considerations of the investment are the level of profit expected and the level of risk. In the base line case the level of profit is the percent interest and the risk is zero.

The quantitative assessment of risk has been avoided by most stock market practitioners. Risk is usually characterized in a subjective manner. An investment might be described as having "low" or perhaps "acceptable" risk. It appears that the overwhelming majority of market transactions are justified by just such a subjective measure. In many situations, the standards are changed to fit the available investments. Such thinking has given rise to index funds which measure their performance relative to the market averages. It is highly possible that an investment is "low" risk when compared to other stocks but a bad investment when compared to a savings account. The subjective approach to risk assessment falls far short of the standards required by the scrupulous investor. The reader may consider the hedges of Chapter VI interesting. But, are they all equally good or even acceptable when compared with the risk free baseline rates?

Judging the quality of an investment is not a simple matter even "after the fact." An investor might compare the rate of return achieved from an investment to the rate of return that would have been received if the money had been deposited in a bank. This approach is misleading on two points. First, it is of little value to discover a bad investment after the money has been lost. And second, it is not clear from the analysis how much luck was involved.

> Consider the investor who plays the numbers game for $1.00 and wins $600.00 on the first day.

By "after the fact" analysis, it appears that playing the numbers game was a good investment since a 600% profit was realized in one day. The annualized rate of return is astronomical when compared with the offering from a saving institution. The odds, however, were not in the investors favor; in the long run, he must come out a loser. There is, however, an interesting corollary to any investment theory. That is:

"No amount of study or planning will ever beat dumb luck!"

The key to risk management of investments is not based on winning big. The key is to develop a method which defines both the profit potential and the risk and to make only those investments which are justified on both counts.

The question then, given that we can determine the profit characteristics, is; "What is the Risk?"

7.2 VOLATILITY.

There is one statement which can be made with absolute certainty about the future price of any stock. That statement is; "The price will fluctuate." Little else can be said with the same certainty about the future. The present price of a security is known and all the past history of both the price and the company is available. There are those who would contend that it is impossible to predict with certainty the future price of a security.

Technical analysts generally will not agree with this position. They feel that by charting the past price movement and by drawing trend lines and support zones that the future can be determined. In answer to this position, I submit that if any investor could consistently predict the future price of a single security that, in a short time, he would be immeasurably wealthy. Many men have searched for the key which will unlock the golden vaults, but it remains as yet undiscovered.

Malkiel* argues that technical analysis cannot succeed. The technical analyst is constantly plagued with indicators which appear to work for some finite period. But in using them, it is never clear when they will go awry. This effect is known to the statistician as spurious correlation.

---

*Note: Malkiel's book (Ref 6), "A Random Walk Down Wall Street" is recommended reading for anyone who is a believer in traditional technical analysis.

Although technical analysis may not be the solution, all is not lost. For although we cannot predict the future based on the past, there are some general statements which might be made. Mathematicians have faced similar loggerheads in their dealings with certain natural processes. The application of probability and statistics is the scientific approach to the characterization of a process which can not be fully described deterministically. Essentially, probability and statistics allows us to make some general statements about the outcome of an undefined process. In effect, we will be able to speak in terms of the probability of a certain outcome without knowing *a priori* what the actual outcome of the process will be.

> Consider the example of flipping a coin on an even money bet.

We have no idea *a priori* whether the outcome will be heads or tails. However, we can state categorically that there are two and only two possible outcomes; heads or tails. And, having flipped the coin a number of times in the past, we can state that each outcome is equally likely.

The reader may feel that the statistical statements about the coin wager are of little value. Not enough is known to insure that a given player will win. In fact, this is a correct observation, but let us not throw the baby out with the bath water. The statistical information is useful because both players are assured that the coin wager is a fair investment.

What then might be said about the future price of a common stock? First, we know that the price of a stock cannot fall below zero but it is unbounded on the up-side. Second, from past experience, we know that a stock is more likely to go up one point than it is to double in price. Similarly, it is more likely to drop one point than to halve its value. Third, the investor is primarily concerned with profit. Therefore, the percentage of change in a stock price is more important than the absolute level. An investor with $10,000 could buy 1000 shares of a $10.00 stock or 100 shares of a $100.00 stock. A 10% move in either stock price would produce the same financial result. Finally, we might contend that some stocks are more likely to double or halve than others. This last point may be restated that; some stocks are more volatile than others. A quick comparison of technology and banking stocks will validate this point. Beyond these statements there is little that can be said about common stock prices which will not be subject to some heated but valid arguments.

The volatility statement is of particular importance. In Chapter VI several hedges were presented. The volatility, or likelihood of a given price swing will, in large measure, affect the profitability of a hedge. Highly volatile stocks will generally work well in the convertible/stock hedge (see Figure 19) because they are more likely to reach the highly profitable points on the profit curve. Conversely, these same volatile stocks may fair poorly in the triangular shaped stock/call hedge (see Figure 13) because their volatility will tend to drive the stock price into the high loss region of the profit curve. Of course, the option premium and the security prices will play a large part in the results of the actual analysis.

The application of probability analysis, while it may be useful, is not a panacea. The theory of probability is a relatively new field when compared with other mathematical studies such as geometry which dates back to ancient times. Probability analysis is normally applied to processes which are to complex or insufficiently understood to permit a deterministic solution. The main issue with the application of probability analysis is one of closeness of fit. In the absence of a deterministic solution, the practitioner is left with little alternative but to select from the limited set of probability tools and apply them to his problem of risk assessment. The criteria of selection of probability tools is constrained by the availability of specific tools and the practitioner's ability to apply them.

The academic community is our best source of now ideas and theories on stock price movement. At the same time, academicians are by nature perfectionists. Their efforts to understand the stock price process are also limited by the same lack of tools within the science of probability. Still, they endeavor to search for the ultimate statistical description of the price movement process.

The investor is constrained by practicality. His ultimate goal is to produce a profit through an improved understanding of risk. It is important to make a reasonable estimate of the risk. It is not necessary that the estimate be perfect.

7.3 A WORD ABOUT MARKET INDICATORS.

Investors have long sought to understand the market in simple terms. In an effort to boil things down to a manageable set of numbers, many different indicators have been developed. Indicators represent an expedient window to the market which is sometimes clouded by their inherent simplicity. Some indicators have a statistical basis while others are linear combinations of factors. The price to earnings ratio is an example of a linear combination factor. Statistical indicators run the gambit from averages to volatility measures. Regardless of the basis of the indicator, the investor is cautioned to fully understand their meaning and limitations before relying heavily upon them.

Perhaps the best known statistical indicator is the Dow-Jones Thirty Industrials (DJ 30) average. The average is a marvelous accomplishment for the statisticians. By judiciously selecting a mere thirty industrial securities, Dow-Jones was able to estimate the average price movements of all the industrial securities on the New York Stock Exchange. The utility of this indicator can easily be appreciated if one sits down with a calculator and tries to compute the full market average by hand. The Standard & Poors 500 (S&P 500) index operates in much the same manner as the DJ 30 but is based on a greater number of securities. Today, computer technology can instantly provide the actual values directly without the error inherent with the use of any indicator. Yet, because of tradition, the Dow is still the most quoted indicator of market performance.

Another of the popular statistical indicators is Beta. Beta is an indicator of the sensitivity of the movement of an individual stock price to the movement of an index. There are several fine points to remember when using Beta. First, Beta is an average of the stock's performance as compared to the market's (i.e. index) performance. A Beta of 1.0 indicates that on the average the subject stock moved the same percentage as the average market share. Beta does not provide a measure of the correlation (i.e. the dispersion) of the security price moves to the average market price. Second, care must be exercised when selecting the source of the market average. Remember, the DJ 30 and the S&P 500 are only indicators of the average price of common stock. While these indicators generally track the average market price, they are not perfect estimators. Third, Beta does not provide an indication of the absolute volatility of a stock. Beta provides a very rough measure of relative volatility to the average share of stock.

In addition to these well known indicators, there are a myriad of others. The quality control and consistency among indicators is highly ambiguous. Volatility is a pertinent example of an indicator which has a host of different definitions. The moral of this discussion is *caveat emptor* (i.e. buyer beware). The investor is admonished to carefully research the source of any indicators and to understand their basis before employing them in his analysis.

CHAPTER VIII

STATISTICAL REPLY

8.1 THE RANDOM VARIABLE.

At this point in the discussion, we come to a major fork in the philosophy of investing. The market's technical analysts will insist that the market's future can be predicted based on its past performance. Specifically, the future price of a stock can be predicted given its past price and volume history. There are others, such as Roberts (Ref 7), and more recently Malkiel (Ref 6), who subscribe to the theory that stock price motion is a random process. The pioneer of this position was Louis Bachelier who developed an elaborate mathematical theory of speculative prices and tested it against the French government bond market of the early 1900's. Since then, the academic community has devoted considerable effort to study the securities markets and the theories of technical analysis. A series of papers on this subject, to include Bachelier's work, has been collected and published by Cootner (Ref 8). The results of these studies raise serious doubt that accurate predictions through technical analysis are possible. The studies demonstrate that an accurate method of technical analysis has not yet been discovered.

The study of the market is far from conclusive, nor is it free from controversy. Even today, it is hard to find a market practitioner who does not believe that by looking at past history of prices one can say something significant about a stock's prospective behavior. At the same time, it is almost as difficult to find an academician who believes that such a backward look is of any substantial value. The academic community is itself far from consensus on the details of the studies. There are, however, certain assumptions which can reasonably be made. Although there are those who can prove any assumption to be invalid in the pure sense, the assumptions to be presented are useful approximations of the real world.

> Consider the problem of selecting a model for the shape of the world.

If you wish only to cross your back yard, the assumption that the world is flat is totally acceptable. If you wish to travel from New York to London, a spherical approximation is required. To place a satellite in orbit, however, requires the earth be more accurately characterized as a flattened sphere. But even with the last approximation, a case could be made that it is not valid and a better approximation can be found. The point is, however, that the model need be only as sophisticated as the application requires. The emphasis should be placed on obtaining an "effective" model, rather than one which is "perfect".

The problem then faced by the sophisticated investor is to analyze the work from the academic community and to boil it down to a useful and effective process for his analysis of *risk*.

To proceed from this point, we must accept the position of the academic community that the market is a random process which can be characterized and modeled in a statistical sense. The question which follows from this assumption is: What then, is the random variable?

There is more than one choice for the random variable (RV). At first guess, the investor might be tempted to select "stock price" as the RV. As it happens, however, this is a poor choice.

> Consider the investment of $1,000.00 in two securities. XYZ company selling at $1.00 per share or ABC company selling at $10.00 per share.

With your $1,000.00 you can purchase 1000 shares of XYZ company or 100 shares of ABC company. As an investor, you are concerned with the growth of your investment rather than the absolute price of the stock. You are equally happy with a 25% up move in either security. In one case this corresponds to a $0.25 move in the price; in the other, it corresponds to a price move of $2.50.

The academic research supports this position, and there is in fact little disagreement that the random variable (RV) is the ratio of stock prices. Given a list of closing prices for 40 weeks, the list of RVs is computed by taking each element and dividing it by its predecessor. Table 18 contains the results of such a process.

To make the analysis manageable, two further assumptions are necessary about the RV. Both of these are subject to very heated debate in the academic community, and neither is completely correct. The issue at hand is not the accuracy of the assumptions, but rather their utility and the resulting closeness of fit.

The assumptions are that the RV is both independent and stationary. These are very strong statements in a statistical sense and should not be taken lightly. The statement of independence which is supported by Osborne (Ref 10) implies that the value of the RV is not affected by any past or future value. In short, all events are independent of the others. Remember, that the RV is the ratio of stock prices and not the price itself. The assumption of stationarity implies that the stock does not change volatility over the period of consideration. This statement can be softened if changes in volatility are slow over the period of interest and can, therefore, be disregarded as insignificant.

At this point, the reader may be concerned with the uncertainty of the process. It hardly provides a warm feeling to know that there are no absolutes. The ultimate intent, however, is to “estimate” the risk in a way which has sound scientific basis. If it could be characterized precisely, there would be no need for statistics in the evaluation. The reader should consider the position that a reasonable assessment of risk is a significant improvement over no assessment at all.

TABLE 18. STOCK PRICES TRANSLATED INTO RANDOM VARIABLES.

WEEK	STOCK PRICE	RANDOM VARIABLE
1	23.750	
2	23.000	0.968
3	23.250	1.011
4	22.750	0.979
5	21.750	0.956
6	20.500	0.943
7	19.750	0.963
8	19.750	1.000
9	19.500	0.987
10	17.000	0.872
11	15.750	0.927
12	16.500	1.048
13	16.000	0.970
14	17.000	1.063
15	18.000	1.059
16	17.250	0.958
17	17.250	1.000
18	17.000	0.986
19	17.500	1.029
20	16.500	0.943
21	17.000	1.030
22	16.500	0.971
23	17.250	1.046
24	16.500	0.957
25	16.000	0.970
26	15.750	0.984
27	16.500	1.048
28	16.000	0.970
29	17.000	1.063
30	18.000	1.059
31	17.250	0.958
32	18.500	1.072
33	19.000	1.027
34	19.500	1.026
35	19.000	0.974
36	19.750	1.039
37	20.500	1.038
38	21.250	1.037
39	21.000	0.988
40	21.500	1.024

TRANSACTION: Weekly Close for XYZ Common Stock.

8.2 THE DISTRIBUTION FUNCTION.

Having defined the random variable as the price ratio, the next issue is to select a probability distribution function which best fits the observed data. Let us approach this problem from the position of an investor's practical experience at the onset and discuss the actual scientific results later.

On the basis of experience, there are several statements which can be made with respect to the price movement of common stock. First, we know that the price can not go below zero, but is theoretically unbounded for an upward move. Second, a 10% move in the stock price is more likely than a 50% move. Third, historically the market in general and stocks in particular demonstrate an upward bias over the long term. Fourth, and perhaps less than obvious, is the statement that the most likely future price for the average security is the current price. The basis for this last statement is the analysis performed at the University of Chicago and stated succinctly by Fugler (Ref 9).

After a careful examination of the available statistical tools, the investor is likely to select the Lognormal distribution function displayed in Figure 20 to model the price ratio random variable. This function possesses all the characteristics described above and has the distinct advantage of being easy to manipulate in the mathematical sense. The Lognormal distribution has these mathematical characteristics because it is based on the Normal distribution or bell curve. The Normal distribution is used by many teachers to adjust the grades of the students in their class in a process commonly known as "grading on the curve." When the RV is characterized as Lognormally distributed, the statement implies that the logarithm of the RV (i.e. $\log_e$(RV)) is Normally distributed and can be characterized by the bell curve. Thus, a second translation of the raw data is in order. Given the closing price of a security for 40 weeks, the RV is computed as the ratio of the weekly prices. Taking the logarithm of these ratios transforms the Lognormal RV into the Normal RV and allows for convenient processing of the probability distribution function. There are a wealth of theorems which apply to the Normal distribution. This simple logarithmic translation of the RV permits them to be applied to our problem. Table 19 demonstrates this translation process for 40 weeks of sample data.

The justification for the selection of the Lognormal distribution model has been addressed in the academic community by Osborne (Ref 10) and Alexander (Ref 11) among others. The consensus of the community appears to support the selection of the Lognormal distribution function. The reader should not be misled, however, to conclude that the controversy is resolved. Several academicians, such as Fama (Ref 12), and more recently Mandansky (Ref 13), have raised objection to the Lognormal hypothesis. A point of departure in their analysis is that while the price ratio's are "close" to Lognormal, they show a consistent tendency for a greater number of large price changes than expected.

The work of Mandansky (Ref 13) finds the distribution distorted from the classic Lognormal form. Specifically, the distribution is higher in the peak and the tails but narrower in the medium price ratio range. From a position of practicality, however, the issue remains one of closeness of fit and utility of application. It is not clear that modifications of the Lognormal assumption, proposed by Fama or Mandansky, will significantly improve the estimate of risk in a financial sense.

For the present, accepting the Lognormal distribution function as the model is reasonable, effective, and has sufficient scientific merit to satisfy the needs of the investor.

RELATIVE PROBABILITY VS. PRICE RATIO.

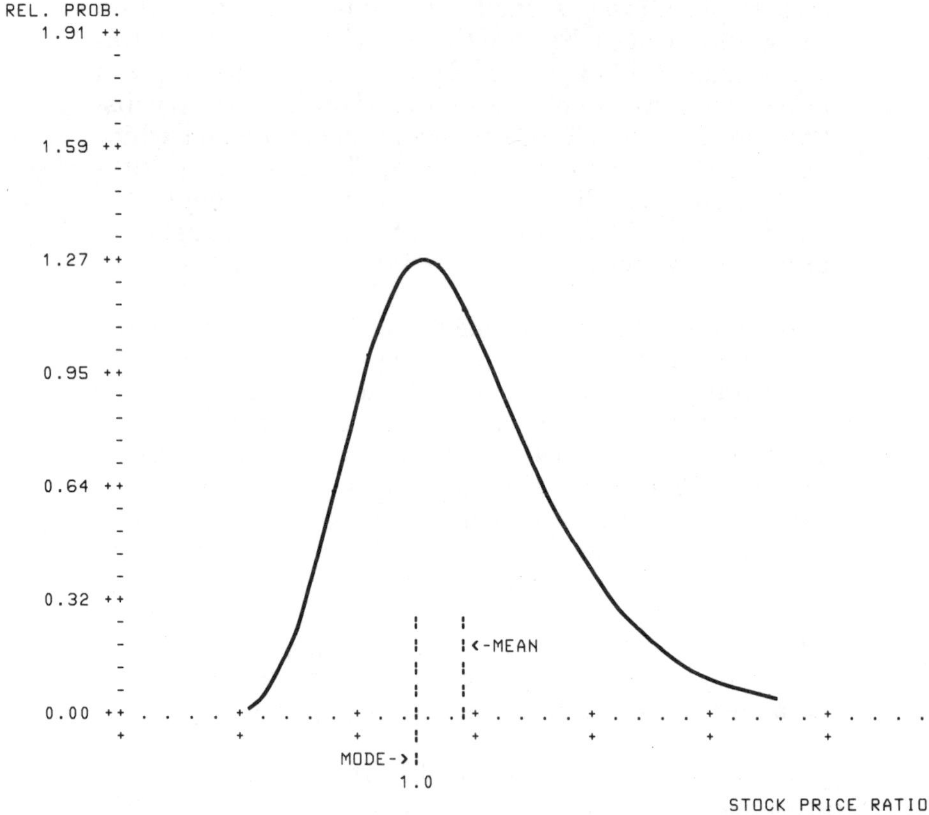

FIGURE 20. PRICE RATIO DISTRIBUTION FUNCTION.

TABLE 19. STOCK PRICES TRANSLATED INTO NORMAL RANDOM VARIABLES.

WEEK	STOCK PRICE	LOGNORMAL RANDOM VARIABLE	NORMAL RANDOM VARIABLE
1	23.750		
2	23.000	0.968	−0.0321
3	23.250	1.011	0.0109
4	22.750	0.979	−0.0217
5	21.750	0.956	−0.0450
6	20.500	0.943	−0.0592
7	19.750	0.963	−0.0373
8	19.750	1.000	0.0000
9	19.500	0.987	−0.0127
10	17.000	0.872	−0.1372
11	15.750	0.927	−0.0764
12	16.500	1.048	0.0465
13	16.000	0.970	−0.0308
14	17.000	1.063	0.0606
15	18.000	1.059	0.0572
16	17.250	0.958	−0.0426
17	17.250	1.000	0.0000
18	17.000	0.986	−0.0146
19	17.500	1.029	0.0290
20	16.500	0.943	−0.0588
21	17.000	1.030	0.0299
22	16.500	0.971	−0.0299
23	17.250	1.046	0.0445
24	16.500	0.957	−0.0445
25	16.000	0.970	−0.0308
26	15.750	0.984	−0.0157
27	16.500	1.048	0.0465
28	16.000	0.970	−0.0308
29	17.000	1.063	0.0606
30	18.000	1.059	0.0572
31	17.250	0.958	−0.0426
32	18.500	1.072	0.0700
33	19.000	1.027	0.0267
34	19.500	1.026	0.0260
35	19.000	0.974	−0.0260
36	19.750	1.039	0.0387
37	20.500	1.038	0.0373
38	21.250	1.037	0.0359
39	21.000	0.988	−0.0118
40	21.500	1.024	0.0235

TRANSACTION: Weekly Close for XYZ Common Stock.

The distribution function can be viewed as a measure of the likelihood of an event. An example of a statistical question concerning an event is: What is the probability that the stock price ratio will be greater than one? Said another way: What is the probability that the stock will increase in value? The area under the distribution function describes the probability that an event will occur. The greater the value of this area, the more likely is the subject event. The distribution in Figure 20 shows that the probability of an advance in the stock price is slightly more than half the total. By definition the total area (i.e. the probability of occurrence of any possible event) is equal to 1.0. This is true because the area under the distribution is greater to the right of the "Price Ratio = 1.0" line shown on Figure 20. This result should not be surprising since we selected the Lognormal distribution with the understanding that stock prices show a propensity to rise in price over the long-term.

Dealing with the Lognormal RV involves the process of translating the RV to a Normally distributed RV (i.e. take the logarithm of the ratio), performing the necessary statistical transformations and translating back into the original RV data space. The nature of the physical process is such that the Normally distributed RV has a zero mean. This feature permits some simplification of the classical equations which describe the process. The reader should note the use of the Normal RV's variance in the equation which describes the Lognormal RV distribution and its mean and variance. The Lognormal distribution function is described by the equation:

$$f(RV) = (1/(RV*SQRT(2*PI*V_n))) * \exp(-(\log_e(RV))**2/2*V_n) \qquad \text{(Eq 8-1)}$$

$$f(RV) = \frac{1}{RV * \sqrt{2\pi * V_n}} * e^{-\left[\frac{(\log_e RV)^2}{2 * V_n}\right]}$$

Where: f(RV) = Distribution Function for the RV, (Price Ratio).

RV = Random Variable, (Price Ratio).

V_n = Variance of the Normal Random Variable ($\log_e$ of the Price Ratio).

In addition to this mathematical definition of the distribution function, three parameters are useful in characterizing the probability distribution and the risk. These are the Lognormal distribution function's mean, mode, and variance. The mean represents the average value (i.e. expected value) of the RV. The mean occurs to the right of the mode, which is the most likely value for the RV. The Mode corresponds to the peak of the distribution function displayed in Figure 20. The position of the mean to the right of the mode is the manifestation of the upward long-term bias in the market. The mean can be evaluated by calculating the first moment of the distribution function or by applying the equation:

$$M_{ln} = \exp(.5{*}V_n) \qquad \text{(Eq 8-2)}$$

$$M_{ln} = e^{\frac{1}{2} V_n}$$

Where: M_{ln} = Mean of the Lognormal RV, (Price Ratio).

V_n = Variance of the Normal RV, ($\log_e$ of the Price Ratio).

The mode of the distribution function is the value of the RV which corresponds to the most likely value for the RV or the peak of the curve. The mode can be computed by applying:

$$MODE_{ln} = \exp(-V_n) \qquad \text{(Eq 8-3)}$$

$$MODE_{ln} = e^{-V_n}$$

Where: $MODE_{ln}$ = Mode of the Lognormal RV, (Price Ratio).

V_n = Variance of the Normal RV, ($\log_e$ of the Price Ratio).

The variance is a measure of the width of the distribution function or the volatility of the RV. The variance can be determined by computing the second moment of the distribution or by applying the equation:

$$V_{ln} = (M_{ln}**2) * (\exp(V_n) - 1) \qquad \text{(Eq 8-4)}$$

$$V_{ln} = M_{ln}^2 * e^{V_n} - 1$$

Where: V_{ln} = Variance of the Lognormal RV, (Price Ratio).

M_{ln} = Mean of the Lognormal RV, (Price Ratio).

V_n = Variance of the Normal RV, ($\log_e$ of the Price Ratio).

8.3 ESTIMATING THE STATISTICAL FACTORS.

To this point, we have defined the RV as the ratio of stock prices. We have also said that the ratios are Log-normally distributed. In addition, and perhaps less than obvious, we have selected the week as the time period under consideration.

The time period selection is also based on a compromise of real world considerations. The candidate alternatives are daily, weekly or monthly time periods. Selecting daily closing prices improves the distribution model, however, the improvement does not compensate for the trouble of handling the additional information. The monthly time period requires that the data cover a long time period to have sufficient data points for an effective statistical model. The selection, then, is driven by the elapsed time and the quantity of sample data. It is not desirable to select an elapsed time which is short because the data may be contaminated by seasonal fluctuations. On the other hand, inordinately long elapsed time periods tend to reduce the model's ability to represent the current volatility of the stock and it also works counter to our assumption of "stationarity." As a rule of thumb, the elapsed time should be in the range of 26 to 52 weeks. In the selection of time period, experience indicates that the weekly period provides a balanced compromise between the quantity of data and the accuracy and effectiveness of the model.

The problem at hand, then, has been reduced to the estimation of the statistical factors which describe the distribution of the RV which is defined as the ratio of weekly closing prices. A good textbook on applied statistics is recommended reading if an in-depth understanding of the process is required. Most of these texts are written to solve problems in diverse fields. The key factor is the realization that we have reduced our problem to a mathematical process performed upon a random variable, the actual application is not important for the time being. An extremely useful presentation of the mathematical process has been written by Krumbein and Graybill (Ref 13) who address the application of statistics to the problems of geology.

The distribution function, f(RV), is described by Equation 8.1. The independent variable of the equation is the price ratio (i.e. RV). The equation requires a security peculiar constant which is the sample variance (V_n). The sample variance is a measure of the volatility of the security based on past price data. The reader should note that this constant is the variance (V_n) of samples of the Normal Random Variable (NRV) (i.e. $\log_e$ of the ratio). In order to apply the distribution function to our problem of risk assessment, we must determine the value of V_n. In our example, the sample set is 40 weeks of closing price data for XYZ company. This data has been translated into 39 samples (i.e. $\log_e$ of the ratio) and is displayed in Table 19. The sample variance is computed by applying the equation:

$$V_n = (1/(n-1)) * \text{SUM} ((\text{NRV})**2) \qquad \text{(Eq 8-5)}$$

$$V_n = \frac{1}{n-1} * \sum (\text{NRV})^2$$

Where: V_n = Sample Variance of the Normal Random Variable, ($\log_e$ of the Price Ratio).

n = Number of Data Samples, (RV Samples).

NRV = Normal Random Variable, ($\log_e$ of the Price Ratio).

Applying this equation to the data in Table 19 yields a sample variance of 0.00211.

The results of the variance computation can be applied to the distribution function equation (Eq 8-1). The distribution function of the Lognormally distributed RV (i.e. the stock price ratio) for the example is defined by the following equation:

$$f(RV) = (1/(RV*0.115)) * \exp(-(\log_e(RV))**2/0.00422)$$

A graphic representation of the computed distribution function is displayed in Figure 21. The mean (M_{ln}), mode ($MODE_{ln}$) and the variance (V_{ln}) of the Lognormal RV can be computed by applying equations 8-2, 8-3 and 8-4 respectively. This is left as an exercise to the reader.

Through the process described above, we have taken a sample of stock price data on a weekly basis and estimated the variance (i.e. the volatility) of the security for a period of one week.

The reader may have some valid questions as to the confidence which should be placed in the estimate of volatility. There are statistical theorems which deal with the characterization of the confidence in an estimate. The application of these additional techniques are discussed by Krumbein and Graybill (Ref 13) and are considered beyond the scope of this text. As a point of reference, it has been my experience that use of 52 weeks of price data provides more than sufficient confidence for our purposes.

Equation 8-5 represents the classical method to estimate the variance of a set of random samples which are Normally distributed with zero mean. Parkenson (Ref 14) has developed a modified approach called the extreme value method which uses the weekly high and low price ratio to estimate the variance of the RV ($\log_e$ of the ratio). This technique appears to have significant merit but will be left as an area of further study by the reader.

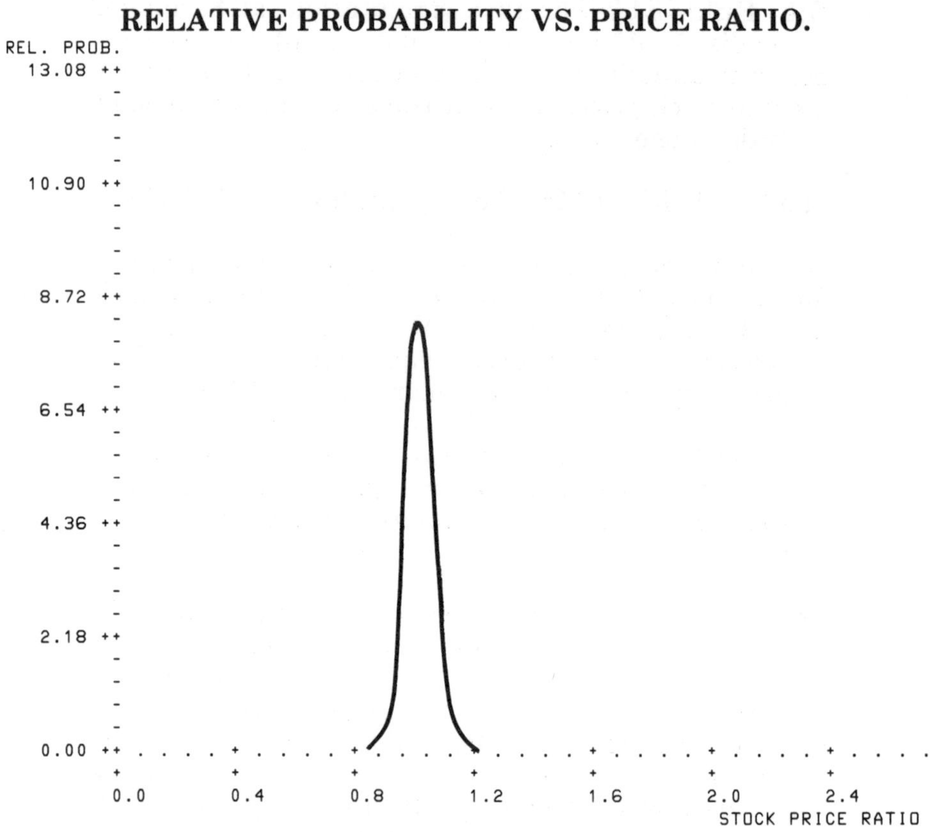

FIGURE 21. PRICE RATIO DISTRIBUTION FUNCTION FOR ONE WEEK.

TRANSACTION: Process 40 weeks of closing price data for XYZ company. See Table 19.

8.4 PROJECTING THE DISTRIBUTION.

Having computed the distribution function for one week's move in the common stock price, it is necessary to project the distribution for a subject investment's duration. The intent of this step is to make the statistical data compatible with the profit characteristics of the investment. The length of this projection is based solely on the securities in the investment. If the investment includes options, the projection is for the time remaining until the option expires. If the investment contains no inherent time constraint, as with the stock/bond hedge, a 52 week holding period is used for convenience.

The process of projecting the distribution is based on the assumptions that the RV is both stationary and independent. Valid concerns can be raised with respect to the application of this projection as the holding period becomes very large. Again, the driving consideration is toward a reasonable approximation. For holding periods of up to two years, this method of projection seems appropriate. The laws of classical statistics provide that the projected variance of a Normally distributed independent RV with zero mean is described by:

$$V_{np} = np * V_n \qquad \text{(Eq 8-6)}$$

Where: V_{np} = Projected Variance of the NRV, ($\log_e$ of the Ratio).

np = Number of Periods, (Number of Weeks for the Investment).

V_n = Variance of the NRV for One Period, ($\log_e$ of the Ratio).

By inserting the value obtained for the projected variance into equation 8-1, the distribution function for the projected time period is defined. There is, however, one more factor to take into consideration. We stated at the onset that the most likely future price of a security is its current price. To this point in the discussion, we have done nothing which will insure that our model complies with this requirement. In order to insure compliance, we must force the peak of the projected distribution function (i.e. the mode) to occur at the RV value equal to one. The simplest method to force compliance is to compute the mode of the projected distribution using equation 8-3 and then bias the RV. The biased random variable is computed by applying:

$$BRV = RV - (1.0 - MODE_{ln}) \qquad \text{(Eq 8-7)}$$

Where: BRV = Biased RV, (Price Ratio).

RV = Random Variable, (Price Ratio).

$MODE_{ln}$ = Mode of the Distribution Function for the Projected RV, (Price Ratio).

The biased RV is used in the distribution equation (Eq 8-1) in place of the RV. The final result of this process is a distribution model which meets the four attributes (see section 8.2, paragraph 2) which were stated at the onset. In addition, the adjusted distribution can be mathematically combined with the profit characteristics in order to estimate the RISK of the investment.

To complete the exercise, let us apply the final equations to the example of XYZ company. We will select the default investment holding period of 52 weeks. By applying equation 8-6, the projected variance (V_{np}) is 0.1100. Using these values in equation 8-3, the mode of the projected Lognormal distribution is 0.8958. Applying this data, equation 8-7 can be reduced to:

$$BRV = RV - 0.1042$$

By substituting this expression for "RV" into equation 8-1, the adjusted distribution function can be described mathematically by:

$$f(RV) = (1/((RV-0.1042)*0.831)) *$$
$$\exp(-((\log_e(RV-0.1042))**2)/0.2199)$$

This equation is plotted in Figure 22 and represents the projected distribution of XYZ common stock prices at the end of the next 52 week period. Two additional points should be made. First, the conversion of the abscissa labels to absolute stock prices instead of price ratios is performed for the convenience of the investor. This transformation is made simply by multiplying the current stock price by each ratio value. A current stock price of $19.00 was used for this example.

Second, the bias adjustment necessary to center the mode at a ratio equal to one (1.0) will also effect the calculations of the mean of the Lognormal distribution. Since the distribution has been moved to the right along the horizontal axis, the mean will also move by an equal amount. In our example, this corresponds to a shift in the mean of +0.1042. The reader should note however, that the variance, which is a measure of the width of the curve, is not affected by the bias adjustment.

8.5 WHAT THIS MEANS TO THE INVESTOR.

On the basis of intuition and academic research, we have concluded that the ratio of security prices is a random variable. Further, we have selected the Lognormal distribution to model that random variable. Unlike the market's technical analysts, we make no claim to predict the future price of a security. Rather, we contend only that a security which is highly volatile will remain highly volatile and a stable security will remain stable. The model allows for both the advance or the decline in the security's price. By applying the laws of statistics, we have established a window through which we may view the likelihood of a move in the price of the security.

The preceding chapters of this text provided the tools necessary to analyze the resulting profit potential of an investment. A myriad of combinations were presented which resulted in a variety of investment situations. These situations were interesting, however, there was no mechanism to judge their worth. By combining the statistical information on the likelihood of an event with its financial consequences, an assessment of the worth of an investment can be made. Our judicious selection of annualized percent profit as the metric allows comparison between investments and the other offerings of the financial community. Since the profit curves of our investment situations are sometimes negative, there is a potential for loss. The statistical model provides a measure of the likelihood that a stock price will move into this negative profit area. We may characterize risk, then, as the probability of a loss.

This capability is of immense value to the sophisticated investor. For perhaps the first time he has, at his fingertips, the means to evaluate the worth of an investment before the fact.

RELATIVE PROBABILITY VS. STOCK PRICE.

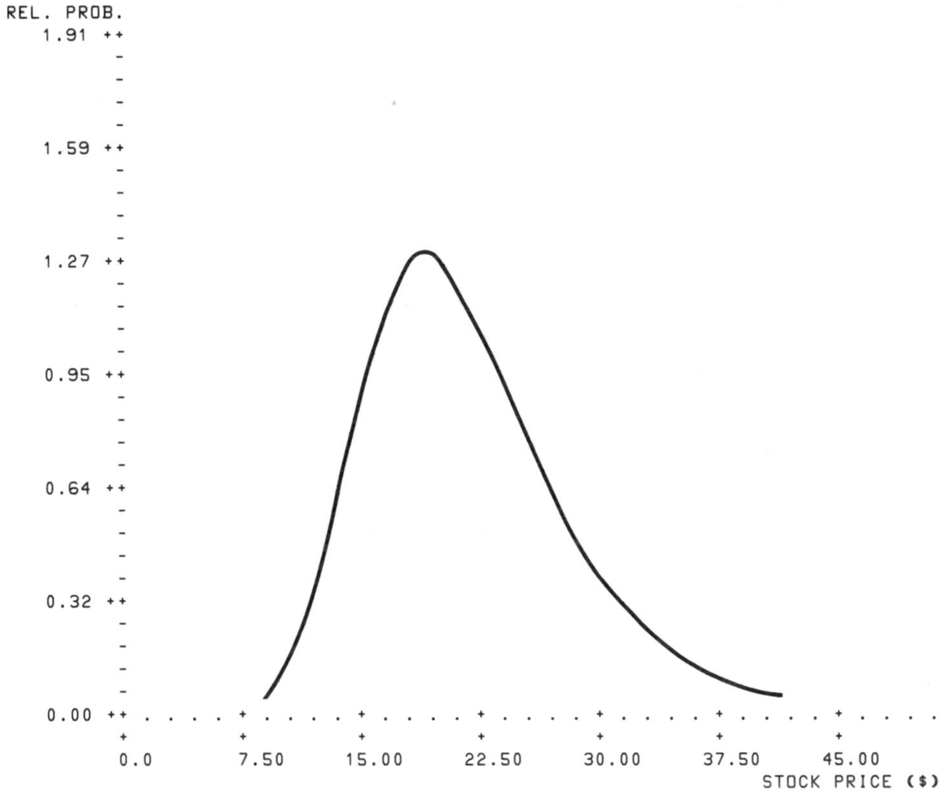

FIGURE 22. PROJECTED PRICE DISTRIBUTION FUNCTION FOR 52 WEEKS.

TRANSACTION: Process 40 weeks of closing price data for XYZ company and project it for 52 weeks. See Table 19. The current stock price is $19.00.

CHAPTER IX

THE MAGIC MIX

9.1 COMBINING THE PROFIT AND THE DISTRIBUTION.

The last step in the analytical process is to combine the profit curves for a candidate investment and the projected distribution of stock prices. There are two ways to approach this problem. The first is the mathematically elegant approach. Under this approach, the equations for the distribution and the profit characteristics are combined and reduced to a simplified expression which is called the closed solution. The second, and perhaps the more practical approach, involves the use of numerical techniques to combine and reduce the input equations.

The Black-Scholes model (Ref 15) is an example of a closed solution of the call option investment. While this model is useful, it is limited in scope for our purposes. The analysis of hedges will require a series of these models to cover the myriad of hedges presented in Chapter VI. On the other hand, the numerical approach to the problem is general in nature since the same processing steps can be applied to the analysis of any hedge. This flexibility is not without implications. As a practical matter, the problem is best solved on a digital computer. If the reader does not have access to computer resources, this technique could be applied manually by sacrificing resolution of the final results. This manual process is both cumbersome and time consuming and is therefore not recommended.

In Chapter VI, the mathematical tools were provided for dealing with the profit characteristics of a hedge. The results of the analysis of each hedge is a table of annualized percent profit (%P) and a graphical representation of the results. Chapter VIII provided the reader with the means to evaluate the likelihood of occurrence of an assumed stock price. This is expressed in the form of the statistical distribution of common stock prices. If care is exercised during the analysis to insure that the abscissa of both the profit curve and the distribution have the same scale factor, the curves can be superimposed. Consider the convertible/stock hedge presented in Section 6.8 combined with the distribution analyzed in Chapter VIII. The combined profit and distribution curves are displayed in Figure 23 for the transaction which is described by:

> Buy 20 XYZ company convertible bonds for $950.00 each. The bond has an investment value of $800.00 and a conversion ratio of 40 shares of common stock. The bond's yield is $120.00 per year. Sell 200 shares of XYZ company common stock at $19.00 per share. The stock pays a dividend of $0.50 per share. The holding period for the hedge is arbitrarily set to one year. The margin interest rate is 13.5% and the entry commission is $270.00. The resulting original value (OV) is $9770.00 with a margin interest charge of $1280.00 for the holding period.

Visual inspection of the two curves will serve to further reinforce our understanding of the expected behavior of this investment.

In this example, we note that the most likely stock prices are concentrated at the least profitable portion of the profit curve. In addition, there are points on the profit curve which are unlikely. In our example, it is unlikely that the investment will yield a profit in excess of 60%.

The original intent of this exercise is to provide a common denominator for comparison among investments and an assessment of risk. Unfortunately, the pictorial combination of the profit and probability curves does not fulfill this need. Instead, there are quantitative answers to a few select questions which will satisfy our requirements.

PERCENT PROFIT AND RELATIVE PROBABILITY VS. STOCK PRICE

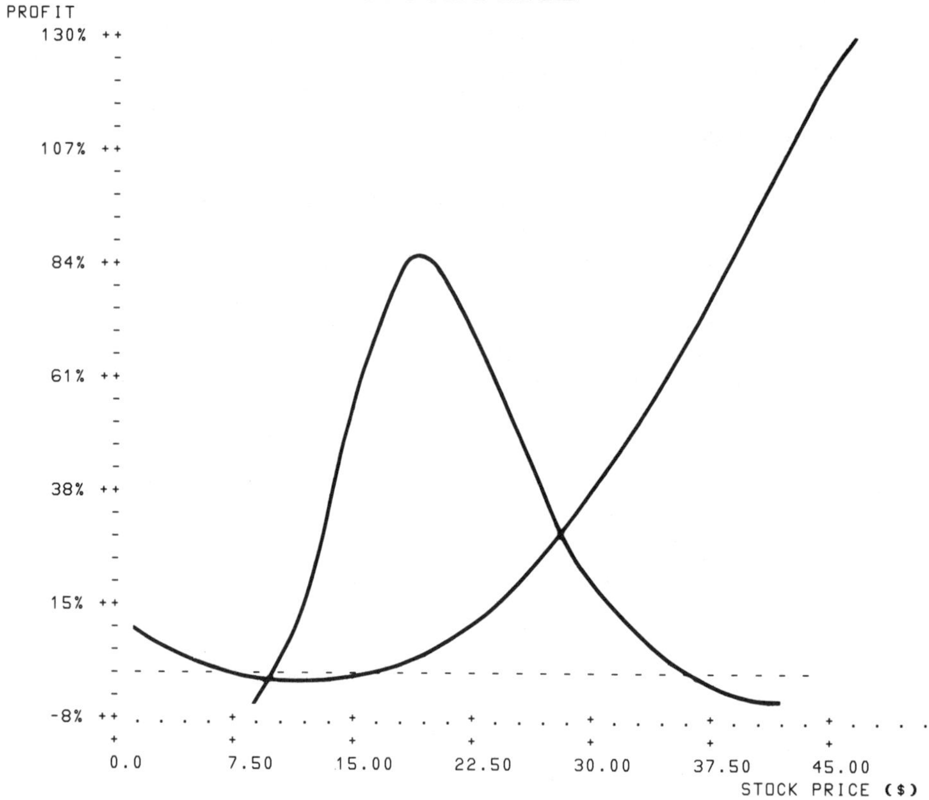

FIGURE 23. COMBINED PROFIT AND DISTRIBUTION CURVES.

TRANSACTION: Buy 20 XYZ company convertible bonds for $950.00 each. The bond has an investment value of $800.00 and a conversion ratio of 40 shares of common stock. The bond's yield is $120.00 per year. Sell 200 shares of XYZ company common stock at $19.00 per share. The stock pays a dividend of $0.50 per share. The holding period for the hedge is arbitrarily set to one year. The margin interest rate is 13.5% and the entry commission is $270.00. The resulting original value (OV) is $9770.00 with a margin interest charge of $1280.00 for the holding period

9.2 BOILING IT DOWN.

The investor is concerned with one very basic aspect of an investment. That is; it's potential to increase his wealth. As a result, the first question which comes to mind in evaluating an investment is, "What is the probability that an investor will profit from this investment?" In the language of statistics, we wish to evaluate the probability of a profit (PP). A second and equally important question which follows is, "What should the investor expect to make from this investment?" Stated in statistical terms, we wish to evaluate the expected profit (EP). Finally, since the actual outcome of the investment cannot be assured, it is important to understand the variability in the return. This variability should be measured relative to the expected profit. The answer to this last issue is expressed by the statistical variable, sigma. The sigma of the profit (SP) is a measure of the range over which the actual outcome may vary from the expected profit.

The reader will recall that it is our stated intent to provide a standard of measure which extends beyond the investment community. It is appropriate, then, to evaluate a baseline investment in a federally insured bank's certificate of deposit (CD).

> Consider the investment in an insured certificate of deposit with Easy Savings for a one year period with a guaranteed 10% return.

Since the account is insured by the federal government, there is virtually no risk of a loss. Therefore, the probability of a profit will be one (PP = 1.0). The expected profit is simply the ten percent annualized interest rate which will be paid on the certificate (EP = 10%). Finally, since the interest rate paid by the CD will not change over the investment period, the sigma of the profit will be zero (SP = 0%).

In the example of a bank's CD, there is no risk (i.e. PP = 1.0). However, the investor may consider the expected profit of 10% to be insufficient. He may choose to seek alternative investments such as a shorter term CD which pays a higher rate of return. However, he does this at the expense of variability in the expected profit (i.e. SP). This is the case because the interest rate may change when the short term CD matures. Alternatively, the investor may choose to accept some risk; that is, accept a probability of a profit which is less than one (for example PP = 0.80). With the additional risk should come an increased value of expected profit and perhaps a change in the sigma of the profit.

These three factors, PP, EP and SP, taken in combination permit the investor to evaluate an investment opportunity and make decisions consistent with his investment strategy. Since most practitioners in the market place do not attempt to make this comparison rigorously, there are periods of time when real bargains exist. It is possible to exploit these short term price anomalies while maintaining an effective frame of reference to the financial community.

9.3 THE FINAL MEASURE.

In order to complete the analysis, the theorems of statistical averages must be applied. These theorems deal with the relationship between a function and a random variable. The techniques are covered in detail by Davenport (Ref 16). The random variable, in our case, is the ratio of weekly stock prices, and the function is the annualized percent profit curve. The thrust of this discussion is to determine PP, EP and SP for an investment which is defined in terms of its profit curve and the Lognormal distribution of common stock price ratios.

The probability distribution function represents the likelihood of the occurrence of a specified stock price ratio. This is presented both graphically and mathematically in Chapter VIII. The probability of a profit (PP) is simply the combined likelihood of all price ratios which correspond to a positive annualized percent profit. By superimposing the profit curve, and the distribution curve a graphical representation of this process is possible. Consider the example investment presented in Section 9.1 and restated here:

> Buy 20 XYZ company convertible bonds for $950.00 each. The bond has an investment value of $800.00 and a conversion ratio of 40 shares of common stock. The bond's yield is $120.00 per year. Sell 200 shares of XYZ company common stock at $19.00 per share. The stock pays a dividend of $0.50 per share. The holding period for the hedge is arbitrarily set to one year. The margin interest rate is 13.5% and the entry commission is $270.00. The resulting original value (OV) is $9770.00 with a margin interest charge of $1280.00 for the holding period.

The shaded area of Figure 24 encompasses the price ratios which correspond to a positive profit. The numerical value of this area is the probability of a profit. The reader should note that transformation between the random variable (price ratio) and an absolute common stock price is made, for the investor's convenience only, by multiplying the random variable (ratio) by the current stock price.

Remember also that a required characteristic of the distribution function is that its total area is equal to one (1.0). Therefore, the value of PP will be a decimal fraction of one.

PERCENT PROFIT AND RELATIVE PROBABILITY VS. STOCK PRICE

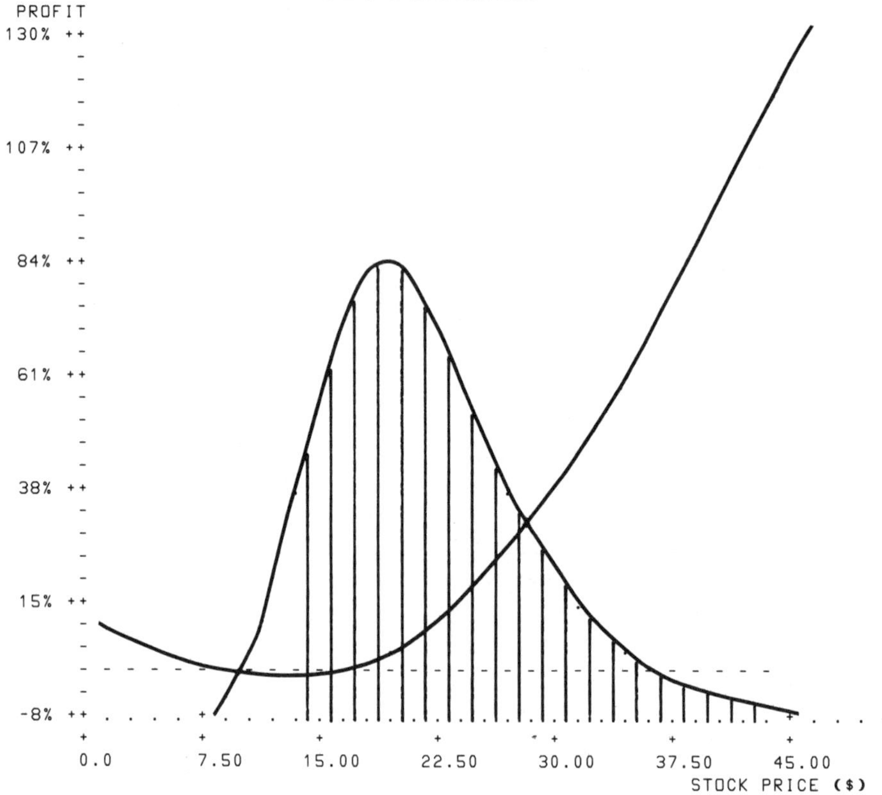

FIGURE 24. PROBABILITY OF A PROFIT.

TRANSACTION: Buy 20 XYZ company convertible bonds for $950.00 each. The bond has an investment value of $800.00 and a conversion ratio of 40 shares of common stock. The bond's yield is $120.00 per year. Sell 200 shares of XYZ company common stock at $19.00 per share. The stock pays a dividend of $0.50 per share. The holding period for the hedge is arbitrarily set to one year. The margin interest rate is 13.5% and the entry commission is $270.00. The resulting original value (OV) is $9770.00 with a margin interest charge of $1280.00 for the holding period

The mathematical definition of PP is described by:

$$PP = \int_{0}^{infinity} f(RV)\,dRV \quad \text{for } \%P > 0 \qquad \text{(Eq 9-1)}$$

Where: PP = Probability of a Profit.

f(RV) = Distribution Function of the Random Variable Ratio. (see Eq 8-1).

%P = Annualized Percent Profit of the Investment.

Equation 9-1 represents the addition of infinitesimally small slices of the area under the distribution function. The rectangles which form the shaded area of Figure 24 are the first level approximation of this process. The result of numerical integration applied to this example yields a value for PP of 0.90. To verify this result the reader should simply view the shaded area in comparison to the total area under the Lognormal distribution curve. If a more rigorous proof is desired, the solution should be pursued by applying numerical integration techniques using the equations for the profit curve and the distribution.

The second parameter is the expected profit. To determine EP we must integrate a composite function which is the product of the probability and the percent profit. This process is expressed mathematically by:

$$EP = \int_{0}^{infinity} \%P * f(RV)\,dRV \qquad \text{(Eq 9-2)}$$

Where: EP = Expected Profit.

f(RV) = Distribution Function of the Random Variable Ratio. (see Eq 8-1).

%P = Annualized Percent Profit of the Investment.

This equation differs from the PP equation in that it is applied over the whole range of possible values for the RV. The reason for this difference is the absence of the test for %P to be greater than zero

If numerical techniques are applied to the solution of EP, the processing is similar to the computation of PP with the exception that each rectangular area is multiplied by its corresponding value of %P. The results of these techniques applied to this example yield an EP of 16%. The reader should note the significance of this process. In effect, it takes into account all possible outcomes of the investment and weights the results against the probability of its occurrence. EP includes the effect of both profit and loss events. As such it is a comprehensive assessment of the anticipated yield of an investment.

The final parameter of interest is the sigma of the profit (SP). SP represents a measure of the variability in the expected profit (EP). This variability can be applied in both directions. That is; it may cause the actual return to be in excess of EP as well as less than EP. This variability is a function of EP and is defined by the expression:

$$SP = SQRT\left(\left(\int_{0}^{infinity} (\%P^{**}2)^{*}f(RV)\,dRV\right) - EP^{**}2\right) \quad \text{(Eq 9-3)}$$

$$SP = \sqrt{\left[\int_{0}^{\infty} (\%P)^2 * f(RV)\, dRV\right] - EP^2}$$

Where: SP = Sigma in the Profit.

f(RV) = Distribution Function of the Random Variable Ratio. (see Eq 8-1).

%P = Annualized Percent Profit of the Investment.

EP = Expected Profit.

The integration portion of the SP equation is performed in a similar manner to the EP process with the exception that the value of %P is squared before the product is computed. The result of this equation applied to our example yields an SP of 20%. The investor should exercise caution when using this parameter. Its meaning is somewhat different than the traditional sigma computed for a Normally distributed random variable. Specifically, its effect relative to a down-side outcome is overstated at the expense of understating the probability of an up-side outcome. With this consideration in mind, however, SP is a useful parameter when comparing investments which are similar in other aspects.

9.4 THE COMPARISON.

And so, we have arrived. In the alternative, we have two investments. The first, an investment in a ten percent certificate of deposit and the other in XYZ company. The results of the analysis can be placed side by side as follows:

	10% CD	XYZ Co.
Probability of a Profit	1.00	0.90
Expected Profit	10%	16%
Sigma in the Profit	0%	20%

In comparing the investments, we note that the CD provides a sure 10% return (PP = 1.0). The securities investment, on the other hand, shows a 10% risk (1.0 - 0.90). The expected profit for the securities investment is higher, but this also comes with 20% variability in the expected return.

In light of the comparison the reader may ask, "Which investment is superior?" Unfortunately, there is no single answer to this question. A great deal depends on the risk and profit objectives of the individual investor. From an independent perspective, these investments stack up about even. The return of the XYZ Company investment is higher, but so is the risk and variability in the return. Let us call to mind the stated objective. That is, to develop an unbiased and common measure of the worth of an investment. This end is served by the proposed methodology which identifies the winners, the losers and the even money investments. The key element in this capability is that the analysis can be performed "up front" where it counts.

9.5 PERFORMANCE.

The application of statistics to the analysis of risk provides the investor with a window through which to base investment decisions. The tools which have been provided permit the investor to evaluate and accept almost any level of risk balanced against an expected return on individual investments. While investment decisions are made individually, their result is realized and measured as portfolio performance. This performance will depend heavily on the criteria which the investor applies during the individual security selection process and the level of risk which he is willing to accept.

This point can be can be best explained using the Capital Market Line which is displayed in Figure 25. The ordinate of this graph is the average annual rate of return expressed in percent and the abscissa is the relative risk, normalized to the average stock market risk. If an investor chooses to purchase treasury bills, the risk is, by definition, zero and the rate of return is essentially guaranteed. As we move to accept more risk, we find corporate bonds which yield, on average, a higher rate of return with the penalty of additional risk. If even higher returns are desired, we find the that investments in common stock have a higher yield but again at the expense of additional risk.

The Capital Market Line is simply a graphical representation of the traditional rates of return which have been experienced in the market place. The reader should note that this is a representation of the *average* performance of the respective investments over many years. On a single year basis, the variability in the rate of return can be significant and is proportional to the risk. It is possible for the rate of return on common stocks to be negative as was the case in 1981 when the S&P 500 average lost over 6%. Table 20 displays the returns during different performance periods for the Capital Market Line benchmark securities. In the recent past, 1978 thru 1982, corporate bonds did not outperform the lower risk treasury bills. This condition is a manifestation of the risk related variability in the rate of return of corporate bonds and the short term of the comparison. The Capital Market Line shows that an investment in common stocks, over the long term, will outperform an investment in the other instruments but it also shows that this is accomplished at the expense of increased risk.

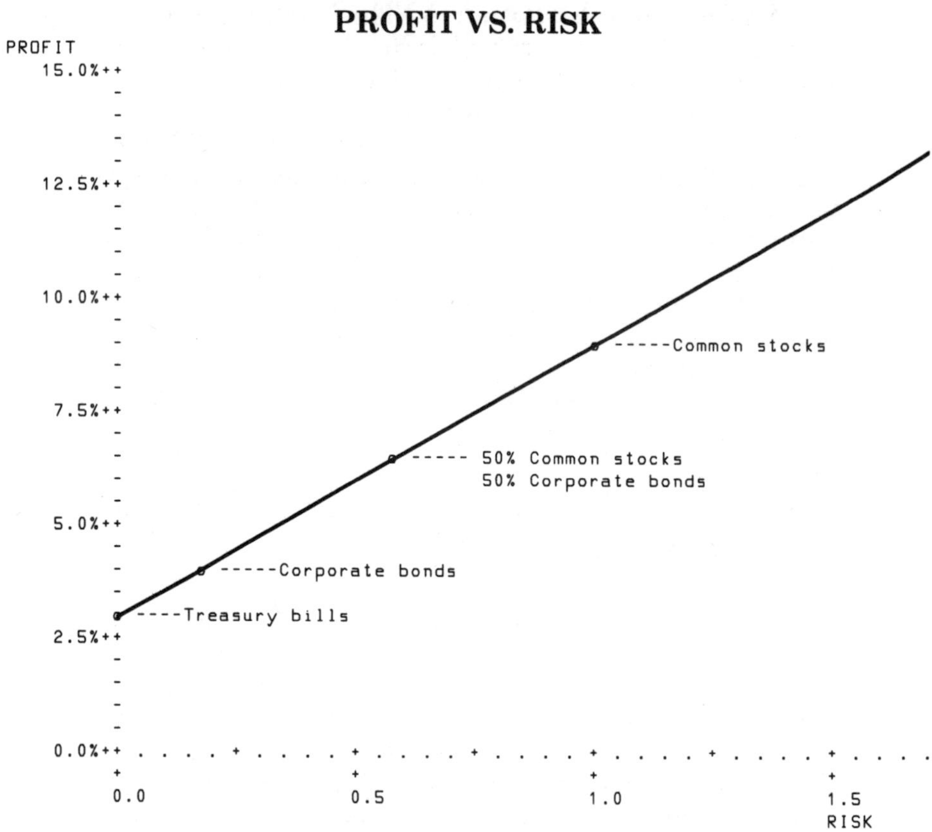

FIGURE 25. CAPITAL MARKET LINE (1929-1982).

TRANSACTION: The graph is based on 57 years of data from 1926 thru 1982 for the respective investments.

TABLE 20. AVERAGE ANNUAL RATES OF RETURN.

	57 Years 1926–82	5 Years 1978–82	3 Years 1980–82
Treasury bills	3.1%	10.8%	12.3%
Corporate bonds	4.2%	5.8%	11.5%
Common stocks	9.3%	14.1%	15.2%

TRANSACTION: Corporate bond data is based on Salomon Brothers High Grade Long–Term Corporate Bond Index. Common stocks data is based on the S&P 500 average which has been adjusted to include dividends.

Risk manifests itself in several ways. In addition to the beneficial effect of increased average returns, increased risk also brings with it increased variability in the rate of return. In terms of the Capital Market Line, we would expect treasury bills to have relatively low variability in their rate of return and the returns from common stock to vary greatly. Historically this has been the case.

The variability in the rate of return taken alone is not a universal measure of risk. But, if we compare investments whose average return is positive over the long term then variability in the rate of return will be an effective indicator of risk.

Ideally, it is the investor's objective to select securities for his portfolio so that his results exceed the rate predicted by the Capital Market Line for the level of risk which he is willing to assume. Again we come back to the question of Chapter IV; "How much is enough?" But now this question has a new dimension, the dimension of *risk*.

In order to discuss the performance of an actual portfolio, we must specify the criteria for the selection of the individual investments. Over the years from 1978 through 1983, the following criteria was used:

> Select only those investments which exceed both a probability of profit (PP) of 0.70 and an expected profit (EP) of 10 percentage points above the available risk free rate.

During this period, selections were based exclusively on the method of risk analysis which has been described. Many of the different hedges presented in Chapter VI were considered and selected. The analysis of a candidate investment also included a limited fundamental analysis in order to avoid companies which were potential bankruptcy candidates.

The results achieved during this six year period are displayed in Table 21. The performance is presented along with the average annual rate of return of the S&P 500 and the treasury bill rates. Figure 26 graphically displays both the Capital Market Line and portfolio performance for the same period. It is significant to note that the results are remarkably close to the selection criteria. The actual rate of return for the portfolio exceeded the risk free rate by just over 10% and the variability in the rate of return, as determined by the standard deviation (sigma), was approximately 40% less than the S&P 500 over the same period.

If we expand the presentation of Figure 26 by one more dimension, we can understand the meaning of the variability in the rate of return as it affects the Capital Market Line. Figure 27 displays the Capital Market Line with the one sigma error ellipses superimposed. The one sigma ellipse implies that 68% of the single year performance measurements will be within the ellipse. As expected, the ellipses indicated a significant amount of instability as we move to accept higher risk. This will cause the Capital Market Line to change slope dramatically if the actual single year returns were plotted. The Capital Market Line, in perspective, is still a valid measure of the average performance of an investment. The error ellipses provide an indication of the stability in the average rate of return indicated by the Capital Market Line.

The actual results of the portfolio are, of course, dependent on the selection criteria. If more risk had been acceptable, then greater returns would have been theoretically possible. The reader is reminded that this text presents the mathematical tools to analyze perspective investments. The actual portfolio performance will be a result of the selection criteria used in the the judicious application of these tools.

TABLE 21. COMPARATIVE PERFORMANCE OF INVESTMENTS.

YEAR	S&P 500	TREASURY	PORTFOLIO
1978	4.6%	7.1%	21.5%
1979	16.4%	10.0%	14.5%
1980	30.5%	11.4%	12.5%
1981	– 7.0%	7.0%	32.7%
1982	19.6%	10.9%	27.9%
1983	20.5%	8.9%	19.7%
AVERAGE RETURN	14.1%	9.2%	21.5%
VARIABILITY	13.3%	1.9%	7.7%

TRANSACTION: Common stocks data is based on the S&P 500 average adjusted to include dividends and a 2% transaction fee. The portfolio performance includes all actual transaction fees which were approximately 4% per year.

PROFIT VS. RISK

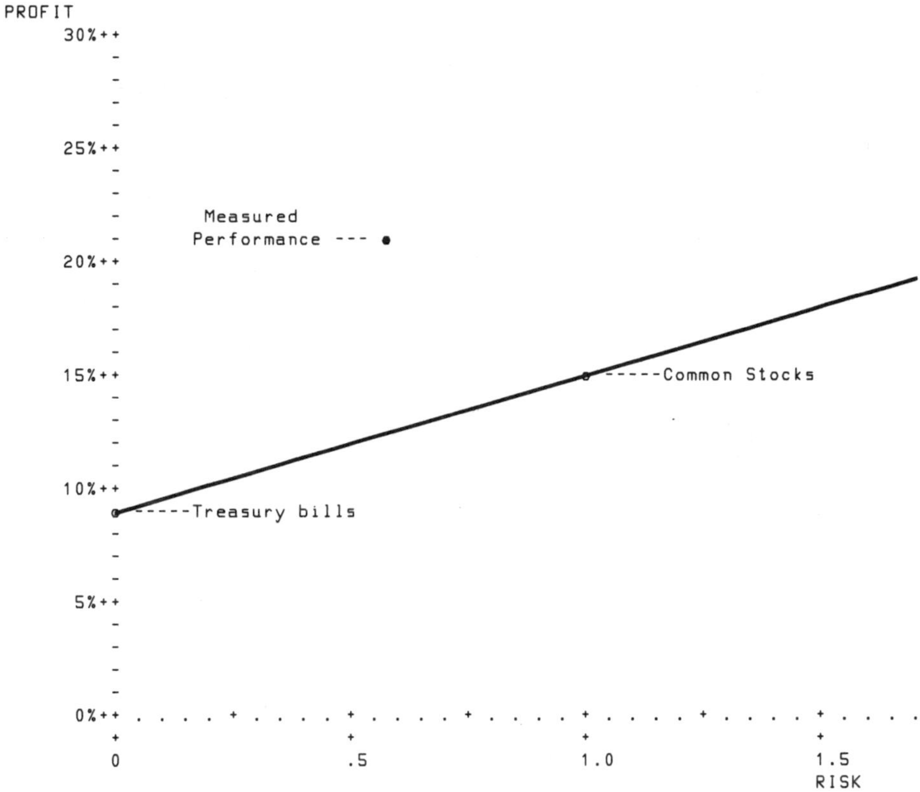

FIGURE 26. ACTUAL PERFORMANCE AGAINST THE CAPITAL MARKET LINE (1978-1983).

TRANSACTION: Common stocks data is based on the S&P 500 average adjusted to include dividends and a 2% transaction fee. The portfolio performance includes all actual transaction fees which were approximately 4% per year.

PROFIT VS. RISK

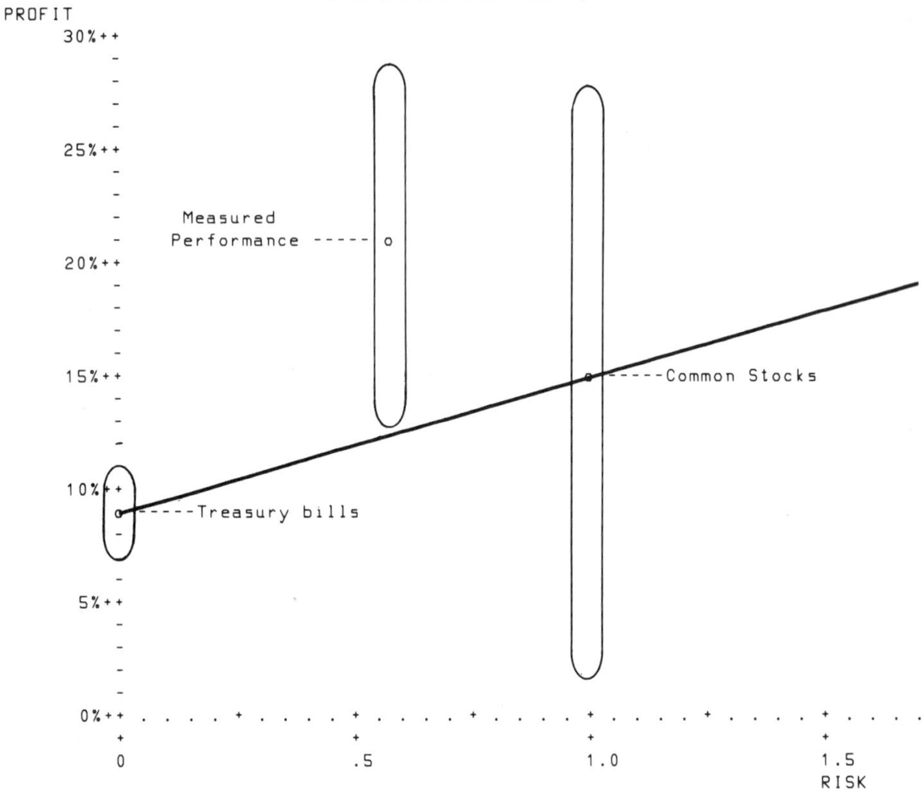

FIGURE 27. THE CAPITAL MARKET LINE PERFORMANCE DISPLAYED WITH ERROR ELLIPSES (1978-1983).

TRANSACTION: Common stocks data is based on the S&P 500 average adjusted to include dividends and a 2% transaction fee. The portfolio performance includes all actual transaction fees which were approximately 4% per year.

CHAPTER X

CONSTRUCTING A PORTFOLIO

10.1 PICK A SECURITY.

The key to winning a horse race is to pick the winning horse. In the market, the investor wins by buying low and selling high. The trick is to find securities which are not fairly valued. These securities provide an edge to the investor. If a security is overvalued, it is a sell candidate. Conversely, if a security is undervalued, it is a buy candidate. Securities which are not fairly valued are the result of both market conditions and regulatory restrictions. Some of the key elements of this phenomenon are: sparse trading of some issues, market anomalies and trading restrictions which are placed on large investors and pension funds.

Hedging techniques can be applied to the process to increase the return on the investment in the most probable common stock price range. This is done at the expense of the profit from the less likely large swings in the common stock price.

The first step in the analysis process is to identify undervalued or overvalued securities. The candidates under consideration are the common stock, the convertible, and put and call options. Of these candidates, the least lucrative source is the common stock. Much of the market is geared to the analysis of the individual issues and trading volumes are relatively high. Investors continuously analyze the information available concerning each company, and the price of the common stock reflects the overall market's assessment of a company's worth. These conditions effectively drive the common stock price to its fair value. The theory which describes this operation is known as the efficient market theory which is addressed extremely well and in practical terms by Malkiel (Ref 6). The reader should note that the key to an efficient market is volume. Securities which are not actively traded may not be fairly valued.

The next candidate form of securities is the option. Put and call options offer some opportunities but these are limited by market competition. This competition is made even tougher by the wide spread use of the Black-Scholes option model. Use of this model provides a quick and accurate method for market professionals to spot options which are not fairly valued. They then buy undervalued options and sell overvalued options until the price advantage disappears. For a professional, this operation can often be done with rapid access to the market and without commission charges. This technique is normally not available to the average investor.

The final candidate security is the convertible. Convertible bonds and convertible perferred stock offer the most lucrative category in which to find undervalued securities. An advantageously situated convertible is one which trades at a price close to both its conversion value (CV) and its investment value (IV). Convertibles in this position, near the corner, will rise with the common stock on the upside but are supported by the investment value for down-side moves in the common stock. If a convertible is trading at the corner, it is a no loss investment. This condition does not occur often. In the absence of this optimum condition, the closer to the corner the better a candidate will perform in a hedge.

The obvious question which comes to mind is, "given this criteria, where should the investor look?" A review of the seemingly endless columns of numbers in the financial section of the newspaper will quickly convince the investor that there must be a better way. As it happens, there is a better way. Special surveys can be purchased which evaluate options and convertible securities. The information is condensed and presented in tabular form for the subject securities. Perhaps the best known survey of this type is the "Value-Line" series which is published by Arnold Bernhard & Co. Inc. These can be obtained on a subscription basis and are available at some public libraries. By carefully evaluating the data published in the survey, the investor can reduce the hundreds of candidates to a reasonable number for full analysis.

There is another discriminator which aids in the selection process. This factor is volatility. In the case of a convertible security, we look first for the convertibles which are close to their corner. Then, based on the hedge under consideration, it is appropriate to consider the volatility of the common stock. The hedge geometry will drive the investor to select a high volatility or low volatility security. Normally in a call/convertible hedge, low volatility is desirable. This is because the profits are concentrated around the option exercise price. Conversely, in a convertible/stock hedge, high volatility is desirable. In this type of hedge, profits are not significant unless the security makes a substantial move in price.

The reader is advised to go back at this point and review the profit curves presented in Chapter VI. When a distribution is overlayed on these curves, the key is to keep the majority of the area of the distribution in a positive profit range of the curve.

A word of caution is in order. The process which has been articulated in this text statistically accounts for the volatility of the common stock. It is based on a rigorous mathematical process. Publishers of market surveys and market professionals often add their own fudge factors to calculated quantities and their processes are subject to change without notice. The investor is advised to be wary of both the source and the quality control of the data which he uses in his full analysis. It is generally acceptable to use survey data, such as volatility, in the initial selection process. However, raw data (i.e., 52 weeks of common stock prices) should be used for the full analysis.

Beyond the process of finding a security which is advantageously situated, the investor must be aware of the overall quality of the company under consideration. There are many sources of this information. Standard & Poors and Moodys represent two of the most respected rating services. Hedging will provide some protection to the investor in the event of the market's reaction to a company's financial trouble. Therefore, it is not necessary to limit the selection process to companies with the highest ratings. However, the investor should make every effort to avoid those companies which are in deep financial trouble. Hedges provide very limited protection in the event of bankruptcy. The bureaucratic nightmare and the resulting delays which tie up funds and prevent the exercise of options can be expensive. A review of the rating services is always recommended especially when the results of the analysis are "too good to be true." A quick glance at the ratings should provide sufficient warning to keep the investor out of trouble.

Convertible securities can have some hidden pitfalls. These occur when the convertibles have special provisions which allow the convertible to be "called" or provide that the conversion provision will expire. The investor should be aware of these provisions if they exist. The "Value-Line" survey provides this information. Normally, convertibles are not "called" unless the company can be assured that they will be converted. This is unlikely to occur unless the convertible is selling for more than 130% of its face value.

10.2 ENTERING A HEDGE.

Once the investor has completed the selection and analysis process, he is ready to enter the hedge. Normally investments involve multiple securities with both a long and a short component. The potential problems occur because of the lack of price concurrency between the component securities. Some small price variations of the component securities can be tolerated. When one of the securities is lightly traded, however, the differential can get out of hand. In addition, the short security transaction provides a potential quirk of its own.

As described in Section 1.1, a short sale can only be executed following an up-tic. In a downward market, an up-tic may be a long time in coming. An investor could potentially lose a great deal of money watching the value of his long position decline while waiting to execute a short sale.

As a rule of thumb, the investor should execute the short sale first. Then, upon confirmation, enter the long position. This rule has an exception when the long security is sparsely traded. In this case the investor should wait for a reasonably stable trading day and execute the long position first.

10.3 CREATIVE TECHNIQUES TO EXIT A HEDGE.

A wise mother once advised her children to "take your tarts when they are passed." One of the benefits of hedging combined with statistical analysis is to identify a reasonable point to exit an investment. Section 4.3 addressed the issue of "how much is enough?" The best advice for the investor is that when that point is reached, it's time to exit the position.

The simplest technique to exit a hedge is to sell the long securities and buy the short securities. This is not the only way to liquidate a position. Since the hedge often involves convertible securities which are trading at conversion value, liquidation can be effected by exercising the conversion privilege. In this case, additional shares are sold short so that the total short position is equal to the equivalent long position. The shares received from the conversion are then delivered against the short position. This technique provides a way to avoid the problems associated with selling a sparsely traded convertible. The conversion process takes some time to execute. Normally, the funds will be tied up for four weeks while the conversion order is being executed. During this period, the movement in the common stock price will effect the debit balance and therefore the interest charges. Depending on the direction of the move, this can be either a beneficial or detrimental effect. The investor must also be careful not to exercise the conversion privilege before the interest is paid. All interest from the last coupon date is usually forfeited upon conversion.

If a hedge involves options, they can be allowed to expire worthless. This will occur if they are below their exercise price. At that point the investor is left with a long position which he may sell or use as part of another hedge. Since the securities are already held, the next hedge does not incur the entry commission to establish its long side.

The stock/convertible hedge has an additional feature. If the common stock declines sufficiently, the short securities can be covered leaving a long position with a relatively high interest payment in a security which is supported by its investment value. If the stock recovers to its original price, the short position can be taken again which will reestablish the hedge. This process leaves the investor with a profit on the original short position. If the price of the common stock advances substantially, an additional short sale can be executed to cover the net long position. If the stock subsequently falls, these additional short securities can be repurchased. This action will generate a profit and reestablish the hedge. Should the common stock continue to rise, the investor can exercise the conversion privilege and liquidate the position with his original profit.

The techniques presented above are provided to stimulate creative thought when it comes time to liquidate a position. They represent an interesting facet of hedging which allows the investor to safely "play" the market swings.

10.4 PORTFOLIO CONSIDERATIONS.

Market professionals have long understood the need to maintain a diversified portfolio. The reason for this is to protect an investor from the unforeseen events which may devastate an individual company or an industry group.

When discussing the risk of a portfolio, two components of risk are in play. The first, called systematic risk, deals with the tendency of all securities to move along with the economy (i.e., the market). The second component of risk, called unsystematic risk, addresses the factors which effect an individual company or industry group. In the absence of unsystematic risk, the risk associated with a portfolio is the aggregate of the risk of each element of the portfolio. The statistical analysis of risk, which is reflected in the value of expected profit, assumes the security is not effected by large unforeseen transients. A doubling of oil prices, for example, would serve as a boom to the oil industries but might devastate the intensive energy user industries. Since there is no way to predict this event in advance, the investor is left unprepared and potentially unprotected from its results. Diversification provides a means to limit the effect of these unforeseen events and thus reduce the component of unsystematic risk associated with a portfolio.

Diversification is a way to avoid putting all your eggs in one basket. However, this approach operates as a two edged sword. If a tender offer is made for XYZ company at double the market price, an investor who is fully invested in XYZ company will profit more than a diversified investor who has only 10% of his capital in XYZ company. On the other hand, the diversified investor is protected from large overall losses if the price of XYZ company stock falls precipitously.

The statistics of our analysis allow for the event of a price increase or decrease within the general range of the price moves in the recent history of the security. On the basis of expected profit of a portfolio, there is no detrimental impact on profitability to diversify. This statement is based on the fact that similar returns can be achieved in different investments. In fact, diversification strengthens the assumption that prices will move in a Lognormal manner. It is appropriate then to seek protection from the unforeseen large transient events through a diversified portfolio.

Diversification depends less on the number of stocks in the portfolio than on choosing companies which have risks related to different economic, social and political factors.

The auto, rubber and steel industries are highly cyclical and are normally affected similarly by the ups and downs of the economy. A portfolio composed only of these industries would have a large unsystematic risk. In the alternative, industry groups such as banks, airlines, computers, drugs, electronics and energy tend to be independent of one another with respect to the movement of the economy.

The obvious question which comes to mind is, "How many securities are needed to reduce the unsystematic risk?" The answer to this question is best provided graphically on Figure 28. As more securities are added to the portfolio, the effect of unsystematic risk is reduced. With five securities, the unsystematic risk is reduced by 80%. By doubling the number of securities to ten, the investor will reduce the unsystematic risk by an additional 10% (i.e., to 90%). As more securities are added to the portfolio, the risk is further reduced but the rate of reduction is slowed. The best the investor can hope for is to reduce the overall risk of his portfolio to the systematic risk level.

The investor is advised to maintain a portfolio of at least five or more securities in unrelated industry groups. This consideration and relatively large odd lot commission costs drives a minimum requirement for capital of approximately $15,000.00 in order to effectively enter the game.

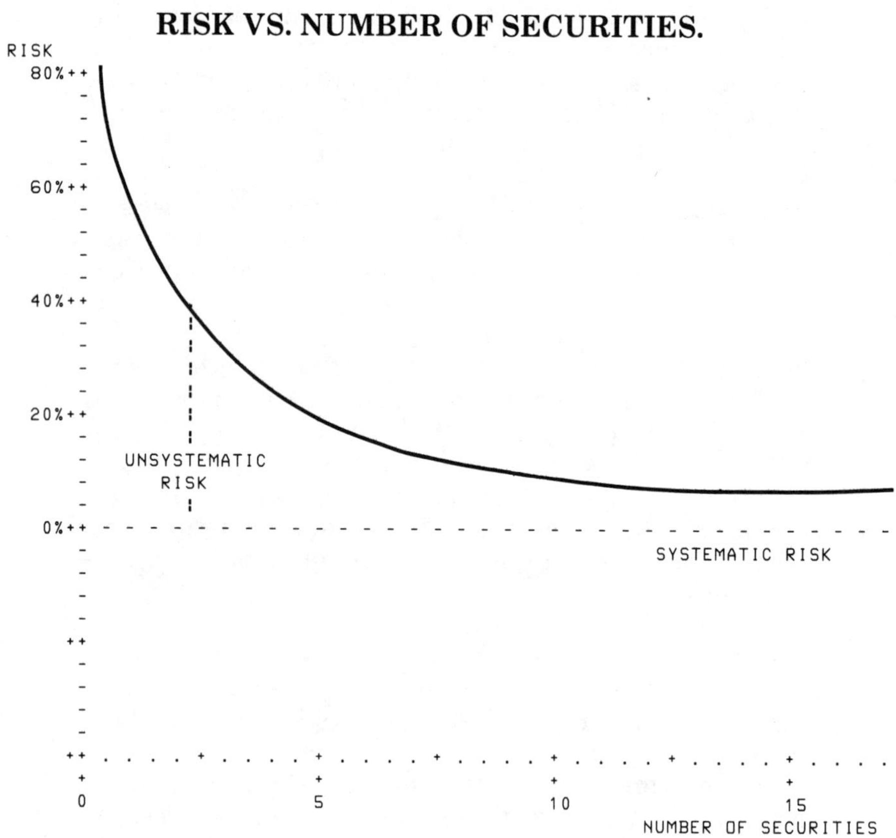

FIGURE 28. PORTFOLIO RISK.

10.5 A WORD ABOUT TAXES.

NUTS!

The governments piece of the action is an important aspect of profitable investments. The situation is one which is constantly in a state of flux with new laws and changing interpretations of the old laws. The investor will be well served to understand the implications of his personal tax situation. It is especially important to appreciate the nuances in the law which may work to his advantage.

With a few exceptions, the tax issues boil down to the question of long term capital gains or short term gains. Hedging often reduces the opportunity for long term gains, but they do not disappear entirely. The method an investor uses to exit a hedge will have the most profound effect on the tax consequences. Therefore, when choosing a method to exit a hedge, taxes should be a consideration.

The complexity and individual considerations of taxes leads me to restrain my coverage of this subject. The reader is advised to further research this subject area. Gastineau (Ref 3) provides a detailed coverage of the tax considerations for options in his book. Mesler (Ref 17) provides a good overall coverage of the subject with an emphasis on hedging. Both of these documents have been overtaken by changes in the tax law. They are, however, a useful starting point. The Internal Revenue Service is the ultimate source of this information. The information is available free of charge but you may find it somewhat difficult to understand.

10.6 HEDGING ASSISTANCE

The investor has three basic options to implement this investment strategy. Each has advantages and disadvantages. The final selection of an approach will depend heavily on both the capabilities and situation of each individual investor.

The first is the "do it yourself" option. Under this approach the investor must perform all the required analyses and issue the instructions to execute each trade. If this approach is selected, it makes good sense to do business with one of the discount brokerage houses. There is a cost advantage to the investor because discount brokers typically charge 40% to 60% less than a full service house. The disadvantage lies in the lack of any support beyond the execution of a trade.

The second option is to "select a knowledgeable broker." In this relationship, the broker will provide guidance and assistance, but the decision authority remains with the investor. Typically, the investor will pay full commission rates on all trades. The value of this service will vary widely from one broker to the next and it may be difficult to find a broker who understands this method of investment. The advantage of this approach is the broker's added attention to the account and his research department's information and analysis. The disadvantages are two fold. First, since the broker's advice will not be implemented in all instances it will be difficult to judge its relationship to either success or failure. Second, the broker makes his money when a trade is executed. Therefore it is to his advantage to recommend as many trades as possible. Even the most scrupulous broker may find it hard to remain unbiased in his buy and sell recommendations. Considering human nature, the best an investor can expect is a broker who recommends trades which are not to the investor's disadvantage. Many of the trade recommendations may be a "wash" for the investor and a source of revenue for the broker.

The third and final option involves a relationship between the investor and an investment advisor. Typically, in this type of arrangement, the investment advisor has the authority to issue buy and sell orders in his clients account. The investment advisor is paid on a "percentage of equity" basis and therefore has no incentive to trade unless it is to his clients advantage. Under this option, the investor should insist that his account be traded at a discount commission rate and managed by the investment advisor. This makes the cost of a standard broker and an investment advisor approximately equal. The advantage of this approach is the centralized account management by a qualified professional who is accountable for the performance either good or bad. The disadvantage lies in the limited control which is exercised by the client and the fee which must be paid regardless of the performance.

The investor might be skeptical of trusting an investment advisor with his capital under these terms. As it happens however, it is the Securities and Exchange Commission which requires payment on a "percentage of equity" basis. This technique discourages high risk investments since the investment advisor makes his living by maintaining accounts and not through a one time windfall. In addition, it is possible to set up an account in which the investment advisor has limited power of attorney. Under this arrangement, the investment advisor does not have direct access to the funds in the account and can only issue buy and sell instructions. These features serve to protect the investor by removing both the reason and the potential for questionable activity by the investment advisor.

10.7 WHERE DO WE GO FROM HERE?

Work on this subject will continue in the academic community. Certainly, the last word has not been written. Noddings (Ref 18) has proposed an interesting extension to traditional hedging in what he calls a "Super Hedge". Under this concept, Noddings maintains that securities of diverse companies are tied loosely to each other and to the market. Hedges can therefore be established in a highly diversified portfolio by buying undervalued convertible securities and selling overvalued options. Since the securities are coupled through the market, on the average, the investor should expect to profit from the aggregate position. While Noddings defines his approach mechanically, he offers little theoretical proof of his assertions. Still, it is an interesting concept which is worthy of further study.

In closing, it is appropriate to state that there is no golden fleece. You have at hand a method to assess the risk in an investment. This knowledge can then be applied to improving the overall performance of your portfolio. It represents a way to see where you are going and to enter an investment with an understanding of both the risks and the rewards.

Good luck with your investments!

BIBLIOGRAPHY

1. Samuelson, "The Rational Theory of Warrant Pricing", Industrial Management Review, Spring 1965, p13-31.

2. McKean, "Appendix to the Rational Theory of Warrant Pricing", Industrial Management Review, Spring 1965, p32-40.

3. Gastineau, "The Stock Options Manual, McGraw-Hill Book Company", Copyright 1977.

4. Prospectus, The Options Clearing Corporation, October 29, 1979.

5. Charell, "A Great New Way To Make Money", Stein & Day Publishers, Copyright 1978.

6. Malkiel, "A Random Walk Down Wall Street", W. W. Norton & Co. Inc., Copyright 1975.

7. Roberts, "Stock-Market 'Patterns' and Financial Analysis: Methodological Suggestions", Journal of Finance, Vol 14 No 1, March 1959.

8. Cootner, ed., "The Random Character of Stock Market Prices", M.I.T. Press, Copyright 1964.

9. Fugler, "Strategy Session", Commodities, September 1976.

10. Osborne, "Brownian Motion in the Stock Market", Operations Research, Vol 7, March-April 1959.

11. Alexander, "Price Movements in Speculative Markets: Trends or Random Walks", Industrial Management Review, Vol 2 May 1961.

12. Fama, "Mandelbrot and the Stable Parentian Hypothesis", Journal of Business, Vol 36 No 4, October 1963.

13. Krumbein and Graybill, "An Introduction to Statistical Models in Geology", McGraw-Hill, Copyright 1965.

14. Parkinson, "The Random Walk Problem: Extreme Value Method for Estimating Variance of Displacement", University of Florida, Department of Physics and Astronomy, September 1976.

15. Black ,"Fact and Fantasy In The Use of Options", Financial Analysts Journal, July-August 1975.

16. Davenport, "Probability and Random Processes", Mcgraw-Hill, Copyright 1970.

17. Mesler, "Tax Planning", Advanced Investment Strategies, Noddings, Calamos and Assoc. Inc., Chicago, Il., Oct 1979.

18. Noddings, "Advanced Investment Strategies", Dow Jones-Irwin, Copyright 1978.

INDEX

NOTES

NOTES